CAN WE ESCAPE?

We spend our lives running from fear and anxiety. Without success. Psychotherapy, drugs, sex, even religion, are only a few of the ways we try to hide from our most naked emotions. Yet all escape mechanisms are doomed to failure. RELEASE FROM FEAR AND ANXIETY offers another route—the route of acceptance. This fear and anxiety can be positive catalysts in our lives if we understand them and respect their power. In this remarkably sensitive and perceptive book, the Reverend Cecil Osborne, author, scholar and spiritual counselor, offers a method for channeling these two God-given emotions into creative energy and liberation from self-defeat.

RELEASE
FROM
FEAR
AND
ANXIETY

CECIL OSBORNE

A KEY-WORD BOOK
WORD BOOKS, Publishers
Waco, Texas

RELEASE FROM FEAR AND ANXIETY

A KEY-WORD BOOK
Published by Pillar Books for Word Books, Publishers

First Key-Word edition published March 1977
Third Key-Word Edition, February, 1978

ISBN: 0-87680-805-4

Library of Congress Catalog Card Number: 75-19908

CONTENTS

INTRODUCTION

Anxiety is a part of life. Without it there would be no growth or development, no progress, either for individuals or for mankind. Anxiety is behind the infant's cry, signaling the need for food, to be changed, or to be held. Anxiety provides motivation. In moderation it is completely benevolent, a gift of God to prevent us from being totally complacent, undisturbed, animated vegetables.

Fear too is benevolent. It is the emotion which triggers a multitude of inner processes into action to prepare the organism for flight, fight, or to freeze. Without the emotion of fear, animals and birds would become the unperturbed victims of predators. Without fear, and the attendant caution it generates, humans could become the victims of everything from disease germs and traffic to the Internal Revenue Service.

In chapters one through eleven I deal with various aspects of fear and anxiety. I hope the reader will gain some insight into the workings of these kindred emotions and discover ways in which they can be used productively instead of destructively.

In chapter twelve, "Release—Methods and Means," I deal with techniques which have been used—some successfully and others less fruitfully—to alleviate excessive anxiety and fear. There are four essential steps in achieving a greater degree of wholeness: awareness, acceptance, action, and abandonment. My earnest hope is that you may become somewhat more aware of your emotions, accept them as a legitimate part of your personality, take suitable action to bring conflicting emotions into a working harmony, and then have patience until the process is completed.

My own ancient anxieties, which at times seemed to be out of all proportion to the situation, have diminished to the point where I can think of them as reasonably normal. It has been hard work, and it's been fun, challenging, and rewarding. Conquering external challenges and obstacles can be very gratifying, but a deeper joy and satisfaction come from discovering the internal difficulties, commonly called hangups, and getting them under control.

I spend my days helping people accomplish this; and I find it tremendously satisfying to observe them growing emotionally and spiritually so that they can face their old adversaries, excessive fear and anxiety, call them by name, and conquer them. May the God of peace grant you this gift if he has not already done so.

Cecil G. Osborne

Chapter 1

FEAR CAN SAVE YOUR LIFE
OR RUIN IT

> *I don't believe in ghosts, but I'm afraid of them.*
>
> MARK TWAIN

Look out!" That shout saved my life. I was inspecting a new building under construction and had just stepped over the threshold. Two carpenters on the rafters directly above me were carrying a twelve-foot long two-by-eight plank. One of them lost his footing, dropped his end, and shouted, "Look out!"

I must have taken but a split second to react, to jerk my head to the left and fling up my hands to break the fall of the plank. Half of the blow was broken by my shoulder; half, by my hands. Aside from a very sore shoulder the next day, I was uninjured. One of the carpenters, shaken by what had transpired, said "That thing was headed straight for the top of your head."

I said, "Yes, I know." I was reasonably calm then. Half an hour later I began to feel the fear.

Fear is a God-implanted survival factor. I had survived because, in a split second, fear had triggered a whole series of automatic responses. In milliseconds the warning shout caused me to react and brace myself for the shock of the falling board. With incredible

11

rapidity the adrenal cortex had released adrenaline into the system, activating other glands, the nervous system, and muscles to prepare the organism for an emergency. In that instant I was quicker and physically stronger than I had been a moment before.

The Creative Side of Anxiety and Fear

Fear can activate and marshal all of the resources of the organism to face a crisis satisfactorily. Fear prepares us for fight or flight. It also stimulates us to lay plans for the future so that we shall not be caught unaware by disaster, food shortage, accident, the police, or by our own consciences. On occasion fear can also immobilize one on dead center. Of the three alternatives —fight, flight, or freeze—sometimes "to freeze" is safer than the other choices.

Fear of consequences prompts us to obey the traffic signal almost automatically. The consequence could be either an accident or a police citation. Fear of hunger prompted the cave man to go in search of meat, and it sends modern man forth to his job. Fear of ending one's days in want prompts one to save for the future and to invest with caution. Fear of failure and consequent shame or disapproval usually causes the student to keep his grades up. In a week's time a typical person may take hundreds of actions which are prompted by some instinctual fear. A careless jaywalker, intent on his own thoughts, looks up to see a truck bearing down on him. Fear galvanizes him into action. In the next instant he is enabled to take action faster than he could have before. The emotion of fear triggers all of the body's defenses to react appropriately.

It is a very complex process by which something alerts the mind—a threatened collision, fear of being trapped in a burning building, or even meeting a person on the street who poses some type of threat. With incredible rapidity the mind classifies the situation, labels it threatening, and sets off the alarm system. Im-

12

mediately the nervous system takes over, and an enormous number of adjustments are made to prepare the organism. Respiration becomes deeper, and the pulse rate soars. Blood pressure rises almost instantly, and the blood supply is directed away from the stomach and intestines to the heart, which can now handle a larger supply of blood and pump it to muscles and lungs. All processes in the alimentary canal cease; the spleen contracts and sends its concentrated corpuscles to predesignated areas. Adrenaline is excreted from the adrenal medulla; sugar is freed from the reserves in the liver; and literally thousands of other things take place automatically without the individual having to give the slightest thought to any of these complex processes. In response to fear or rage, this marvelous transformation takes place in an instant to prepare the individual for a crisis.

Modern man seldom faces a saber-toothed tiger. His defenses are more likely to be in response to being chewed out by the boss or to the scores of lesser situations which do not involve a crisis but keep the body's defenses in a super-alert condition. Thus we have an organism prepared for fight, flight, or freeze, but often none of the three takes place. The subject sits stewing in his own (literal) juice consisting of excess adrenaline and other glandular secretions. The stage is set for symptoms ranging from a headache to a heart attack.

Many people are so sensitively attuned that it may not require a threat of any magnitude to set off the alarm system. It may be a thought, a memory, a movie or TV program, or a reaction to a news broadcast. If no physical action is taken after the body's defenses are alerted, the body chemistry is so severely altered that in time various physical or emotional symptoms may occur. It is somewhat like holding the accelerator all the way down but keeping the car in neutral or a foot on the brake—racing the motor and going nowhere, but using up energy and wearing out the motor.

13

Defenses We Use

We have some automatic and largely unconscious defenses against certain standard fears. It may be profitable to take a look at a partial list of an almost limitless number of defenses which are quite commonly used to protect us in response to the emotion of fear (see chart). This list could be extended indefinitely, it is intended only as a short check list so that one may discover how he responds to some everyday fear-inducing situations.

FEAR OF	TYPICAL RESPONSES
Inferiority, shame, or failure	*Passive defense:* withdrawal, giving up. *Aggressive defense:* achievement via acquisition of money, property, badges, titles, degrees, social standing.
People	*Passive defense:* retreat, withdrawal. *Aggressive defense:* attack, criticism. acquisition of social graces.
Death	*Passive defense:* denial—refusal to think about it. *Aggressive defense:* preparation for death, intellectually and spiritually; facing it realistically; frantic activity.
Love	*Passive defense:* retreat, withdrawal, cynicism. *Aggressive defense:* sexual aggressiveness, control of others, compensation or overcompensation in some field of endeavor.
Sex	*Passive defense:* denial of feelings, retreat, sundry distortions, frigidity, impotence. *Aggressive defense:* Don Juanism ("scalp collecting" on the part of either sex), frenzied activity.
Emotions	*Passive defense:* denial, rigidity of personality, emotions, attitudes. *Aggressive defense:* overstressing the intellectual side of life, compulsive behavior.
Future	*Passive defense:* anxiety transferred to the entire organism, causing generalized tension; compulsive eating, drinking, or working. *Aggressive defense:* hoarding, miserliness, acquisition of money or property.

Phobias	*Passive defense:* obsessive-compulsive thinking and behavior; avoidance of threatening situations. *Aggressive defense:* substitution of other activities for the thing or things feared.

No effort is made here to distinguish between creative and destructive defenses. Man is not really a rational being so much as a rationalizing being. When we feel more secure adopting a given course of action, we automatically begin a clever process of rationalizing the decision or action so that it will seem logical. The choice of a defense is nearly always an unconscious process.

"Perfect Love Casts Out Fear"

Some Scriptures seem to imply that a true believer will be without fear. Among the favorite passages quoted is, "Perfect love casts out fear" (1 John 4:18, RSV). This is a spiritually and psychologically sound principle, but it was not intended to suggest that we can or should always be fearless. The Apostle Paul, whose great love chapter has inspired millions, writes to the Christians at Corinth that "I was with you in weakness and in much fear and trembling" (1 Cor. 2:3, RSV). The twelve who spent three years or so walking with Jesus and absorbing his spirit all fled in fear for their lives at the crucifixion. However, after Pentecost they presented another face to the world. They courageously faced the authorities and fearlessly chose imprisonment or death rather than surrender their faith.

I was in the hospital visiting a man who was to be operated on the next day. He joked about the upcoming surgery, but his laughter seemed a little excessive. After a bit I said, "You know, if I were in your place, despite all that I know about the probabilities favoring a successful operation, I think I would be a little tense, maybe scared."

My friend looked thoughtful. "Really? I thought

15

Christians were supposed to be without fear. 'Perfect love casts out fear' and all that."

I said, "Never mind what we're *supposed* to feel. I feel whatever I feel. I get scared at times. It seems fairly normal to me to feel some anxiety before an operation."

"Yeah. Maybe it's normal. Come to think of it, I had a restless night. I woke up thinking about the operation. They do lose some patients with an operation of this kind. Maybe I'm scared and haven't admitted it to myself."

"Then in that case," I replied, "maybe the best solution is to be honest about it, and say, 'Lord, I'm frightened; just plain scared. It's normal. Most people are before an operation. I want to turn this whole thing over to you, without pretending to you or to myself that I'm fearless.' "

"Yes! That sounds about the way I really feel. I think I can pray that in sincerity along with a genuine plea for guidance for the surgeon."

Three Steps to Effective Prayer

Honesty with oneself, with God, and with others is the all-important first step in effective prayer. For that matter honesty (another term for awareness) can be the first step toward the solution to many problems. Step two is acceptance, and step three, abandonment.

Awareness means to get in touch with what you really feel, to let suppressed or repressed feelings come to the surface. To suppress a feeling is to be aware of it without expressing it; to repress a feeling is to deny its reality even to yourself. If you feel fear, or love, or hate, or loneliness, or jealousy, there is no point in denying the reality of the emotion. The feeling doesn't go away just because it is denied. The emotion must be allowed to enter awareness.

Acceptance, the second step, does not imply approval. It involves the simple step of acknowledging the feeling or the situation as a fact. Denying its reality is futile. If repressed into the unconscious mind, it will simply fester and carry out its ugly work of causing emotional or physical symptoms. William James, the father of modern psychology, once said that the most important step in solving a problem is *to be willing to have it so*. That does not mean that one must be content for it to continue indefinitely, but *for the moment* the fact, the *is-ness* of things, must be accepted.

Abandonment means to give up the negative emotion or the problem to God. One could use the term *release* or *surrender,* but for many the word *abandonment* has the more positive connotation of giving the unwanted emotion, attitude, or situation to God and walking away from it. Because spiritual and emotional states are never permanent, it may be necessary to do that often, perhaps five or twenty times a day, until the emotional structure has become convinced that the thing has actually been abandoned.

What about "the fear of God"? I can still recall an incident when I was about seven or eight years old. It was Sunday, and the sermon that morning had been on the text, "The fear of the Lord is the beginning of wisdom" (Ps. 111:10 RSV). My father said thoughtfully, "You know, I'm not *afraid* of God." I wondered if he were going to be struck down for his blasphemy. I was very much afraid of God because the idea had been hammered into me for years. No one ever bothered to explain that the fear of the Lord meant the kind of reverence for God which leads to obedience because of the realization of his power and love.

When Mary Magdalene and the other Mary went to see the sepulchre on that first Easter morning, an angel sought to calm them: " 'Do not be afraid; for I know that you seek Jesus who was crucified. He is not here; for he has risen, as he said. . . . Then go quickly and tell his disciples that he has risen from the dead, . . .' So they departed quickly from the tomb with fear and great joy" (Matt. 28:5-8, RSV). Thus they felt mingled fear and joy despite the angel's kindly admonition not to be afraid. Fear, reverence, awe, and wonder are just clumsy words used to describe a whole galaxy of fragile emotions.

I think I can say that I do not fear God, but I do experience the emotions of awe and wonder, love, reverence, and adoration; and I fear the consequences of disobeying his universal laws. It is not his anger that I fear, but my own weakness. I fear the emotion of guilt that overcomes me when I realize that I have wandered or disobeyed, but that fear is then engulfed in awe over the fact that his love is greater than my sin, and that I can never stray beyond the scope of his limitless love.

A Conditioned Response

According to some standard texts on psychology, a child comes into the world with just two fears—fear of falling, and fear of a loud noise. There seems to be some evidence that a third fear is also inborn—the fear of being abandoned. Instinctively, the infant senses his helplessness, and if someone does not care for him or hold him, he sets up a cry of fear and rage. Thus, fear is a survival factor with which we come into the world.

The first six or seven years, as nearly everyone knows, comprise the most important period of life. In those early years the personality is formed but not finished. The way a person acts at twenty or seventy bears a distinct relationship to what transpired in the first six years.

I saw a dramatic illustration of this in the home of a friend whom I was visiting. In the home were two greatly loved dogs—a tiny poodle and a very large German shepherd. I was astounded to see the big dog cringe when the poodle barked an imperious command. Whenever the poodle wanted the big shepherd out of the room, he had only to bark once and the larger dog meekly obeyed. I asked about their strange behavior.

My friend explained that the poodle had been the

only pet for some years. Then the German shepherd puppy was introduced into the family. At this point the poodle was larger and ruled the roost. He ate first and had the best places to sleep. The shepherd learned to take second place. Now that he was far larger and could have swept the poodle aside with one huge paw, he still obeyed the nervous, authoritarian demands of his tiny friend. He was the victim of a conditioned response originating in his infancy. Theoretically a conditioned response can be reconditioned. In time a good dog trainer could teach the shepherd to stand his ground. The same can be said of humans: We can change and modify early childhood conditioning though we can seldom completely eradicate it.

As a child I had a monumental fear of people. Through the years it diminished until I was rarely aware of the deep-rooted fear, but occasionally now, when I let down the defenses I have carefully built up, I can feel something of the primal fear. It does not rule my life. I manage adequately, but the roots of the fear are still there. When I was four, my hand was cut severely. It healed in a week or two, but the scar remains. Emotional scar tissue remains too wherever there have been deeply rooted fears or circumstances which have left profound impressions.

Most of the unhappy or threatening circumstances in childhood are repressed, that is, buried deeply in the unconscious mind. We know this is true because many buried memories can be dredged up under hypnosis, with the use of sodium pentathol, or in other ways. On occasion I have used not only hypnosis but music therapy and sometimes primal or in-depth therapy, to help people uncover important repressed material (see chap. 12 for a more detailed description of in-depth therapy). Sometimes, though the memory of an event is retained, the emotions surrounding it are repressed. By reliving the experience the individual can often be released from the continuing damage being done by the primal "hurt."

A Primal Experience

A young woman·in one of my Yokefellow groups related a terrifying experience. When she was about seventeen, a young man at a party offered to take her home. As they were leaving the party, three other boys joined them. The four youths then drove to an abandoned rock quarry and announced that they were going to rape her. At that moment another car turned in to the rock quarry, and at the sight of the headlights, the four young men panicked, raced away, dumped the girl out near her home, and drove off. She related this with a certain intensity but with a smile on her face.

I asked, "What are you feeling right now?"

"Nothing. That happened over ten years ago." She was still smiling.

"What did you feel that night?"

"Oh, I was scared out of my wits!"

"Did you ever tell anyone?"

"No, this is the first time I've told about it, except to one very close friend."

"You've told us recently about your generalized anxiety, a sense of insecurity, which is with you constantly. I wonder if that experience you related could have some bearing on your all-pervasive anxiety."

"Who knows? I'll probably never know."

"We could find out. Want to try?"

"Sure."

I led her to a table in the corner of the room, facing away from the group, and asked her to close her eyes. Slowly I started counting backward from twenty-seven, her current age, down to seventeen, from time to time asking her to relax. At seventeen I handed her a foam-rubber bat and told her to start hitting the table, eyes closed. (A dozen other methods would have worked just as well.) As she beat on the table, the fixed smile faded. Then I said, "You are in a car with four boys. It's turning into the rock quarry! It's dark! They're going to rape you!" She hit the table one resounding blow and let out a piercing scream of terror that could have been heard half a mile away. She screamed again and again. Then she stopped and began to tremble violently. I held her and motioned for others to come. We held her in silence while she reexperienced the terror of that night. After a few minutes she began to breathe normally and looked up with enormous relief. The nervous smile she usually wore was replaced by a look of quiet serenity as though a great load had been lifted. She had kept that terror-filled memory to herself, not daring to tell her parents. She had carefully buried all feelings about the event though of course she could recall the experience.

Out of Sight, Out of Mind?

"But why bring it all up again, when it was so safely locked away?" someone asked me once when I related the incident. I explained that basically there is little wrong with any of us except "hurts"—damaging experiences or influences in childhood and subsequently —if we bury those hurts, we are denying to ourselves that they exist, but the inner self knows differently. The repressed emotions are down there in the unconscious mind carrying on their nefarious work of creating generalized anxiety and causing havoc by promoting psychosomatic illness, depression, and any one of a hundred kinds of personality malfunctions.

In childhood we learn to turn off our feelings in order to survive. In adult life we have to get in touch with those feelings in order to live fully. Anger, for instance, displeases mommy and daddy; so in order to survive—to win and keep their approval—we repress the anger or any other emotion that brought a frown to their faces. Now, as adults, those primal hurts and repressions need to be brought to the surface, relived, and discharged.

Both the home and school conspire to wipe out a child's spontaneity and render the child unable to experience normal feelings. When parents forbid the child to have and express emotions such as fear, love, hate, wonder, and jealousy, he or she learns to deny these feelings and pretends not to feel them. In a sense he anesthetizes himself so he cannot feel the pain of rejection. In not being allowed to be himself, he tends to lose his identity. He doesn't know who he is, and this creates a great deal of anxiety.

I had known Doris for over five years and had worked with her off and on during much of that time except, when in a petulant rage, she withdrew briefly into her shell. Doris had a wretched childhood. She felt totally unloved by her parents. If only a fourth of what she related to me is true, she had every reason to feel utterly rejected.

When I first met her, she was about twenty-six, a rather pretty, terribly shy, but determined young woman. She was so hopelessly immature that she could not hold a job, and her marriage blew up after eight months. She was so demanding and so petulant that eventually almost everyone gave up on her. I had her in a therapy group for a year or two and saw her irregularly in counseling sessions. I could see no progress whatever. Finally it became clear to me that *she could not grow up* and accept adult responsibility because she was still unconsciously *determined to remain a child*. Her fear of growing up was based upon a legitimate need to be "reparented." Never having had parental love or care, her "inner child" was still desperately in need of being loved and cared for. She was caught in a bind. Her damaged inner child lived in an adult body, and people expected her to act like an adult, something she couldn't do. Inwardly all she wanted was to be taken care of.

I could not meet her needs. Three different psychiatrists to whom I referred her failed to do so. I had her switch to a woman counselor; results were negative. We tried different types of therapy, all unavailing. She united with a church, was baptized, and attended regularly. She held daily conversations with the pastor, trying desperately to get enough love and support to satisfy her anguished, unloved little inner child. Doris's fear of growing up and assuming adult responsibilities was so great that she may never mature unless someone or a couple can reparent her—take her in, care for her, love her, nurture her, and let her grow up emotionally in a loving atmosphere over a period of years. She will probably remain in her child ego-state unless or until that happens.

I felt a little less frustrated when I read recently that an eminent psychoanalyst likes to have his patients see him five times a week for four to five years. At the end of that time they reexamine the situation to discover whether the patient should change psychoanalysts!

Chapter 2

FEAR—RATIONAL AND IRRATIONAL

> We are troubled on every side, yet not distressed; we are perplexed, but not in despair; Persecuted, but not forsaken; cast down, but not destroyed (2 Cor. 4:8—9 RSV).
>
> ST. PAUL

I've chased more burglars than anyone I know. Just why our house should be selected as a haven for burglars, I am not quite sure; but for many years I was aroused in the middle of the night by unmistakable footsteps. I would awaken, sit up in bed, and listen. The steps would cease. The intruder was obviously waiting for me to go back to sleep. My wife seldom heard the noises, or if she did, attributed the rhythmic steps of prowlers to a banging shutter.

"We don't have shutters," I would tell her.

"Then it's the cat," she would reply.

"Our cat ran away, remember? Probably he couldn't stand having his sleep interrupted by burglars."

But she, an irritatingly sound sleeper, would be asleep again, leaving me to defend our home against the incessant assault of stealthy prowlers. On the average of once a month or so I would be aroused by footsteps or by a door being opened in a sinister fashion. No one in his right mind could mistake those sounds. They were the distinct noises of night prowlers.

Since I could never go to sleep for an hour or so once I had been awakened by a noise downstairs or in an adjacent room, I would arise, turn on all the lights in the house, and explore the premises. I was always faintly surprised and a little disappointed that I never turned up a burglar. Most likely they heard me coming and swiftly departed. They have a way of doing that, you know. They dislike being confronted by a householder whose fear they could easily mistake for righteous indignation. It was not that I exhibited great courage in inspecting my castle at three A.M., with the intent of driving out intruders; it was simply that my intense dislike of lying awake listening for another creaking footstep was greater than my fear. No one relishes the idea of confronting a panic-stricken thief in the middle of the living room, presumably armed and ready to fight his way out of the house. I was no exception.

In the back of my mind I knew I was being absurd. I knew it partly because my patient wife kept reminding me of it. Logically, I knew this was true. I had been chasing prowlers for years and had never succeeded in cornering one. The evidence all pointed to the inescapable conclusion that I had a "burglar neurosis," or "burglarphobia."

One night, after searching the house and finding nothing amiss other than a rhythmically flapping shade in the bathroom, I lay awake trying to discover the roots of my irrational fear. It would undoubtedly have started in childhood. I let my mind flow back through the years to ten, eight, five—Ah! five! Our home in Oklahoma City had been burglarized while we were all away on vacation. We came home to find the house in turmoil. Dresser drawers had been pulled out and emptied in the middle of the floor, closets ransacked, and as I recall, the whole house was a mess.

The family was not in what could be termed a state of prosperity at the time, and the total net loss would not have exceeded five dollars; but from the excitement

26

the burglars caused, one would have thought that the crown jewels had just been forcibly removed from the Tower of London. It was the sole topic of conversation for weeks. Neighbors were regaled with all the details. The probable means of entry were analyzed and argued about. Finally the argument concluded when my father, not noted for accepting divergent views gracefully, announced that the burglars had come through the front door which my mother had carelessly forgotten to lock when we left. (He was later proven to have been the last out of the house, but by that time he had altered his hypothesis so that it became clear that the intruders had climbed through a bathroom window.)

At any rate, I had been traumatized by all of the semihysterical to-do over a simple burglary, the net results of which must have convinced the burglar or burglars that robbing homes in the lower-middle-class sections of the city was a highly unprofitable venture. So it all started at age five. Then I recalled that for several years afterwards when the family returned home late at night, as my father put his key in the lock of the front door, I would always take out my pocket knife, open it, and prepare to fight my way through the surging mass of burglars who would undoubtedly try to flee from the darkened house. It sounds ridiculous, of course, but surely no more so than the months of semihysterical adult chatter about a very unremarkable burglary which had no doubt been committed by some neighborhood boys.

The Source of Overreaction

Most overreactions in adult life and nearly all phobias and/or abnormal fears have their roots in childhood. Adults may know intellectually that the child from one to six is an incredibly sensitive receptor, instantly ready to pick up any impression and record it on the mind's photographic plate for all time, but adults forget. The younger the child, the stronger the impression. The young child has little or no basis for judgment, and normally takes in as gospel or reality even the most ephemeral experience. Discovering the origin of the burglar phobia helped enormously to relieve the situation. I haven't heard a burglar in many years now, and while my sleep is not that of a serene and placid child, I no longer have a problem with night noises.

A Freudian psychoanalyst would have a field day with my burglar experiences. Without delving too deeply into my psyche, I can see that there were other psychic components: a mild anxiety neurosis which formed the fertile ground into which the burglar-seed fell, there to germinate with great fecundity. There were generalized fears, caught by osmosis from parents and peers, and a mixture of amorphous anxieties having no basis in fact. If nothing else, these provided a psychic drive enabling me to accomplish some things which a slothful component of my personality might have sabotaged. So, I can accept the Apostle Paul's dictum, "Give thanks in all circumstances" (1 Thess. 5:18, RSV).

Irrational fears, or phobias, do not always yield to insight; simply discovering the origin of our neurotic fear may not automatically cure us. If someone had pointed out to Hetty Green that her excessive fear of poverty had its roots in childhood experiences that had nothing to do with money, it would almost certainly not have cured her neurosis.

Hetty Howland Green, who died in 1916, left an estate of $95,000,000. She had a balance of $21,400,000 in one bank alone. Her son, who later inherited her fortune, had to have a leg amputated because of Hetty's long delay in finding a *free* clinic where he could be operated on without cost. Hetty lived largely on cold oatmeal, being too stingy to use fuel to cook it. With a fortune of $95,000,000 this seems to most of us to be somewhat bizarre behavior, but to her it seemed quite rational. Perhaps a few years of psychotherapy might have alleviated some of her irrational fear of poverty, but surely no one could have talked her into spending money for a regular hospital if a free clinic could be found. The reason, of course, is that there is no direct connection between logic and emotion.

Eradicating a Phobia

A woman with whom I was counseling stated that she had an abnormal fear of driving which had persisted for several years. She not only feared driving but experienced considerable anxiety when riding with her husband. Rather surprisingly she had not seen any relationship between the onset of her phobia and an event which occurred about five years before. She, her husband, and three children had just driven onto the freeway. As the car reached a speed of about thirty miles an hour, one of the younger children opened the back door and fell out. The screams of the other two children alerted the father, who jammed on the brakes. Both parents rushed back to the child, who had fortunately not been struck by the cars behind them. Though badly bruised, the child had no broken bones and in a few days had fully recovered.

As we delved into the experience, I could sense that the mother felt, not only a sense of shock over the incident, but considerable guilt over not having had locked the rear doors of the car. She had not let her feelings of guilt come to the surface until we discussed it. After some weeks of dealing with the accident and her feelings about it, she seemed to derive great relief. Her drawn, tense face relaxed. Her posture altered. Instead of sitting rigidly in her chair she appeared much more at ease. But in subsequent sessions it developed that she still could not drive although riding in a car with her husband driving seemed much less threatening.

It is a generally accepted fact that removing a symptom without getting at the underlying cause may result in changing symptoms. For instance, through hypnosis, people have been relieved of one symptom only to have another—and often worse—symptom develop. A physician friend of mine related an interesting experience. While treating a patient for a minor ailment, he observed that the man had a serious tic. Once every four or five seconds he would jerk his head violently to the left. Inquiring about it, the physician was told that it had begun two or three years before. My friend, who utilized hynosis in childbirth and for certain other purposes, offered to try to remove the symptom. The patient proved to be a good subject, and in three or four sessions was completely relieved of his tic. A week or two later he phoned the doctor in a panic: "Hey, Doc, you've got to do something. I'm drinking myself to death. It started a day or two after you removed that tic of mine by hypnosis."

The physician had him come in for a further discussion. He said, "Under hypnosis you can tell me, if you wish to, why you developed that tic. I'll show you some finger signals so that you can indicate, while under hypnosis, whether you want to reveal it to me and whether you want me to restore the original tic. Your unconscious mind knows the truth."

Under hypnosis the patient indicated by signals that he was ready to reveal the origin of his tic. He began to talk. It all started, he said, when he decided at age sixty-two that he would leave his wife when he retired at sixty-five. Since making the decision, he said, he had not been able to look his wife in the eye and unconsciously averted her gaze. The sense of guilt carried over into his relationship with other people. Asked under hypnosis whether he wanted the symptom restored or transferred to some other symptomatic expression, the man said that he would settle for the old symptom. The physician restored the original tic, the man sat up, and within the next few minutes was jerking his head convulsively around to his left shoulder. Apparently he preferred that to the prospect of spending the remainder of his days with his wife—a choice with which the physician did not presume to argue.

In the case of the woman who still feared to drive despite insight into the cause of her fear, I felt that since she was fully aware of the origin of the phobia it would be safe to remove the symptomatic behavior. During a number of sesssions, under hynosis she was given the "right" to drive again. The guilt was dealt with, and I gave her absolution, under hypnosis as well as in her normal state. Since false guilt nearly always has its roots in the unconscious mind, it is often much easier to give absolution—assurance of divine forgiveness—under light or deep hypnosis rather than in the fully awake condition.

Any Christian is empowered to give absolution, having been so authorized by Jesus. He said to the apostles, "Receive the Holy Spirit. If you forgive the sins of any, they are forgiven; if you retain the sins of any, they are retained" (John 20:22-23, RSV). While there are differing interpretations of the latter part of that statement, the first portion is quite clear. The apostles, and presumably any of their followers who felt qualified, were authorized to announce the remission of sins.

To rid a person of long-standing deeply rooted phobias can be extremely difficult. In a sense a phobia, or any irrational fear, is a defense mechanism arising out of deep-seated anxiety. The roots can go back to earliest infancy, and the farther back they go, the more difficult it is to deal with them. Some types of grass can be killed easily. Bermuda grass, as I learned to my grief, has roots that can reach down as far as three feet. It can be killed only with great difficulty. In the same way, some phobias of a fairly mild nature can be eradicated without too much difficulty. Others, of long standing and originating early in life, are much more difficult to cope with. In the last chapter, as we deal with various types of therapy, we will consider some of the means by which irrational fears and other symptomatic behavior can be eliminated.

Irrational Mass Delusions

Around the middle to the end of the tenth century, an epidemic of mass fear gripped millions of people. Terror struck the minds of Europeans as a number of fanatics roamed various countries predicting the end of the world and preaching that the thousand years prophesied in the Revelation would end with the coming of Christ who would appear in the heavens to judge the earth.

According to the prophets of doom the last judgment would take place in Jerusalem. Gibbon and Voltaire have both described the mass fear that seized the populace. By the hundreds of thousands pilgrims began the long trek to the Holy Land to await the coming of the Lord. Many of them sold all their possessions and, if they managed to reach the Holy Land, lived there on the proceeds. Knights, citizens, and serfs joined the great migration eastward. Every manifestation of nature was looked upon with fearful fascination. A thunderstorm sent them all to their knees. Meteors brought people into the streets to weep and pray.

It must be remembered that at this point in history not one person in a hundred could read. Superstition and ignorance spread like a black pall over Europe. Rumors assumed the validity of the gospel as fanatical preachers vied with one another in spreading the news of impending doom. In some communities, business was at a virtual standstill for a time.

From the end of the tenth and into the eleventh century, a number of wild, fanatical, but eloquent preachers began to speak about the need to liberate the Holy Land from the hand of the infidel. Religious leaders, including various popes, joined in the chorus, and after the first wave of enthusiasm swept Europe, Pope Urban II began to encourage the masses to launch a crusade to free the Holy Land.

Peter the Hermit led one of the very first Crusades. Crowds of men, women, and children, numbering an estimated one hundred fifty thousand, surged eastward. Most of them had not the faintest idea where the Holy Land was. At every new, strange city they would ask, "Is this Jerusalem?" To condense a vast and unbelievably tragic story, upwards of one-half million people, including those in the Children's Crusade, perished in attempts to reach the Holy Land. Peter the Hermit arrived alone in Jerusalem, his horde of followers having died along the way of hunger, disease, and armed conflict.

How can such a thing happen? It occurred partly because the only religion these people knew was the religion of fear. These miserable serfs, with a very real and vivid fear of hell, responded to the papal promise of forgiveness of all sins—past, present, and future. Mass hysteria engulfed them as they yielded to the promise of forgiveness, of eternal life, and of excitement and to the glory of participating in a great and noble cause. So much for hysteria and mass fear in the Dark Ages.

In the enlightened twentieth century, during the early days of radio, Orson Welles's broadcast of a fictional invasion from Mars created panic and mass confusion over a large part of the United States. Perhaps no age is totally immune to mass hysteria, given the right conditions.

Fears—Ancient and Modern

As a small child I was dreadfully afraid of the dark. I have no idea what factors induced this abnormal fear, but certainly it did not help when my father, in a valiant if misguided effort to rid me of the fear, sent me repeatedly into dark rooms to get something. His assurance that there was nothing in there to harm me did nothing to alleviate my terror.

With that kind of background I have always enjoyed the story of the small boy who was told by his father one dark night to go and get the broom just outside the back door. The boy said, "I'm afraid. It's dark out there."

His father replied, "Don't be afraid, son. The Lord's out there, and he'll not let anything happen to you."

Whereupon the boy went to the back door, looked

out rather timorously, and said, "Lord, if you're out there, will you please hand me the broom?"

Black symbolizes evil and danger. "It was a dark and stormy night" is not a felicitous description with which to launch a cheerful story. Such phrases as "a black heart," "dark plots," "shady deal," and "dark and sinister" carry an emotional impact that bears no relationship to logic. Undoubtedly fear of the dark is as old as the cave man's fear of unknown dangers lurking in the night.

Dark symbolizes the unknown, one of man's basic fears. A child's first day at school, a young person's anxiety on the first date, that first day on a new job—these and many other firsts rank in a sense with Columbus's fearful first journey into the unknown. Historians and romanticists may picture a stalwart and fearless Columbus surrounded by cringing, superstitious sailors, but the facts are that Columbus—for all his determination—had plenty of misgivings. He would not have been human otherwise. We know how the story ends, but he, in his tiny ship, was surely tormented with the fears and uncertainties attendant upon a journey into uncharted waters. No, Columbus was not fearless. Courage is not being without fear; it is going on in spite of fear. A human would not be normal if he did not experience fear in the face of obvious danger, for fear is a God-implanted safety-survival factor.

Hitler is reported by his biographers as having had a number of abnormal fears and phobias. He was afraid of horses, moonlight, microbes, anesthetics, and premature death. He also had an all-pervasive fear of being poisoned. His fear of assassination was so great that generals were required to remove their swords before being admitted to conferences with him.[1]

Millions of otherwise perfectly normal people have phobias or some minor irrational fear. Some phobias originate in adult life, but more often they are rooted far back in childhood.

I had been vaguely aware for many years that I disliked heights, but I had not the faintest idea that the feeling was full blown enough to be called a phobia. I discovered the extent of my phobia on my first plane trip. What I experienced in that small, unpressurized plane twenty-five years ago was not fear. It was sheer panic. There was nothing *under* us. That was all I could sense. I rode from San Francisco to Seattle frozen by a paralyzing fear the entire way.

On the trip back (I had been tempted to return by train, but my schedule would not permit), I experienced the same panic, only to a slightly lesser degree. Approaching the landing field was sheer torture. There was nothing under us but water, and we were coming down. So, remembering William James's "act as if" principle and his concept that "feelings follow actions," I took another plane trip, and another, and another. Eventually I managed to recondition the conditioned response, and in the process of logging some hundreds of thousands of miles by plane, I lost my fear of flying. But my basic, underlying fear of heights remains. I conquered the situational fear, but not the original fear underlying the phobia. Fortunately it poses no problem.

The Fear of Falling

Psychologists and psychiatrists differ on this matter as they differ about many other things. But from both subjective and objective evidence I think it is safe to say that in my case the fear of heights had its origin in a childhood fear of falling below parental standards, below God's requirements, and below my own expectations. Falling, at a feeling level, equals failure. Notice some of the common phrases we employ: "falling from grace," a "fallen woman" (it is interesting that we do not speak of fallen men), and "falling short."

In infancy and childhood, failure to perform properly is usually followed by either some form of punishment, or rebuke, or the withholding of love. To the child this is devastating. He has fallen from his place in the family and is consequently that much less secure.

35

He may experience a sense of guilt and feel anger at his parents for punishing him and at himself for failing to measure up. The fear of falling, then, can be a displaced emotional symptom. Instead of dealing with the moral, spiritual, psychological, and emotional aspects of one's failure—real or imaginary, small or great—one unconsciously transposes his fear of "falling from grace" onto a fear of falling, or a fear of heights, which is the same thing. It is somewhat less threatening, because it is more socially acceptable, to admit to a fear of heights than to confess to a sense of moral and spiritual failure.

Obsessive-compulsive Behavior

Obsessive-compulsive and/or phobic behavior are related. People with full-blown phobias often develop a pattern of obsessive thinking or compulsive behavior as a defense against certain repressed emotions or experiences. However, this is not always the case. At times an individual who may not have a phobia will develop obsessive thinking and yield to compulsive patterns of action. There is always the possibility, however, that the obsessive-compulsive behavior masks the phobia so completely that it is totally obscured.

Jennifer, an attractive and intelligent young married woman, seemed to have no particular phobia, but she was driven to distraction by obsessive thinking. Bizarre thoughts crossed her mind repetitiously, maddeningly. Weird thoughts of self-destruction or of doing herself some injury came to her mind. "Just put those crazy thoughts out of your mind," her logical husband told her. "Don't think thoughts like that. Keep yourself busy with other things and they'll go away. Why do you let yourself be tormented with those absurd ideas?"

Being rebuked by someone who had never experienced the daily torture of obsessive thinking made her feel all the more guilty; and since there is usually some aspect of guilt—real or false—in obsessive thinking, her husband made her feel still more guilty and inadequate. As Freud has pointed out, "The sense of inferiority and the sense of guilt are exceedingly difficult to distinguish."[2] Whether a sense of guilt or a sense of inadequacy lay at the root of her difficulty makes little difference since they are so closely related.

In counseling sessions, and later in two years or more of a group experience, Jennifer made a number of important discoveries. She had what I termed a "princess syndrome." It had its roots in her childhood. Until her sisters were born, she was the princess, the adored, beautiful little girl upon whom parents and other relatives lavished their love and praise. She was pretty, intelligent, cute, wonderful—the ultimate, as she was assured over and over. Then came other children, competitors for parental love. But Jennifer remained the princess; she was held up to her siblings as the ideal toward which they were to strive. She became the model, the lovely, beautiful, perfect child after which the others were to pattern themselves. "Why can't you be more like Jennifer?" she recalls her parents saying repeatedly to her sisters. To make matters worse, she was given no limits. Without guidelines a child tends to feel unloved. She made up her own rules, out of some vague moral and social sense derived by an alert mind from her surroundings. Both parents were employed, and little Jennifer was permitted to grow up more or less on her own.

Considering these various factors, it is surprising that she functioned as well as she did. She had a high ethical and moral sense and accepted responsibility for her own actions; yet, along with these fundamental qualities, she had a "little girl" personality. Some facets of her personality had never been permitted to grow up. In fact, most of her obsessive thinking was similar to the minor obsessive-compulsive behavior which often appears around puberty. Many of her obsessive thoughts had to do with sex, distorted in numerous ways.

In counseling I told her that while obsessive-compulsive behavior was difficult to eradicate, she could be helped, particularly if she would also participate in a group experience. Accordingly I put her in a Yoke-fellow group consisting of ten persons. In private counseling she gained some insight into her problem. In the group experience, over a period of two years, she began to grow emotionally and spiritually. She had a sound religious background and was a faithful church attendant. She also attended a weekly women's Bible study group, but she sensed that something was lacking in her traditional Bible study, good as it was. In the group experience she discovered the missing ingredient—honesty, undergirded by love. Occasionally anger would flare. On one or two occasions she was able to express her anger, and at other times, to be on the receiving end of it without crumpling. But far more important, there was understanding and loving acceptance in the group.

Honesty As a Prelude to Growth

Eventually Jennifer's husband joined the group. For the first five or six weeks he was a typical defensive, intellectualizing, advice-giving member. Finally, gently, lovingly, ruthlessly the group let him have it.

"Ben," someone said, "I like you, or what there is of the real you that shows, but you're a phony. You haven't shared an honest feeling the entire time you've been coming. I'd like to know more of you, so I could like the rest of you too. Why don't you take off that phony mask and let us see who you are?"

"Hey look!" Ben said, "I'm as honest as I know how to be. In my business you don't show your emotions. I'd be a dead duck if I opened up and let people see what I'm really like. Anyhow, I'm not sure who I really am. Give me time. I think I'm beginning to get the idea, but I can't open up all at once. I don't know how."

And in time he did open up. His growth was gradual but spectacular in terms of honest self-awareness and self-acceptance. Ben and Jennifer shared feelings with each other in the group that they had never been able to communicate before. Their candid, open, honest expressions were sometimes painful but always helpful and therapeutic. Their communication at home improved because they had learned in the group how to communicate. In addition both of them discovered a clever little game Ben had been playing unwittingly. He had repeatedly told Jennifer that he wanted her to be independent and self-reliant, but it became obvious to the group and to Jennifer that he was doing everything he could to manipulate her into a dependent position so that he could control her.

It took Ben some time to see this and still longer to change his behavior. Out of some of the pain of discovery and change they eventually developed a much more mature relationship. And in the process, Jennifer did become more self-reliant. She decided to complete her college work and prepare for something she had always wanted to do. In the process she found that the more creative she became, the less her obsessive thinking surfaced. "It's still there vaguely in the background," she told me a year or so after she had moved away and left the group, "but I can control it. It doesn't control me now." She is living a happy, creative, fulfilling life. The old fears are mainly memories which surface from time to time, but they no longer make her miserable.

Chapter 3

FEAR OF PEOPLE

The event may be in the past, but the hurt is in the present.

C. GILLETTE

Most people will experience difficulty in identifying with Katy and her almost unbelievable fear of people, but all except pathological personalities experience a degree of timidity, inferiority, or shyness, if not downright fear, under some circumstances. So Katy's story does have a bearing on our everyday, "normal" fear of people. If Katy could make it, anyone can.

She had asked one of my associates, with considerable uncertainty, if I would see her for a few minutes. When she entered my office and introduced herself, I extended my hand. She stood with her hands behind her back, apparently rejecting my overture. I asked her to sit down. She was obviously very frightened.

Her story, related to me over a period of weeks, was this: Her father had disappeared when she was very small. When she was about four, she watched with horror as her mother shoved a lover down a long flight of stairs. The fall killed him. From then on Katy's life was a nightmare. Her mother said, "If you ever tell anyone what happened, I will kill you!" To reinforce her threat, the sadistic mother used a large leather strap studded with metal to beat little Katy.

In the next few years she was regularly beaten with fists, sticks, and the metal-studded strap. All of the mother's insane fear of a murder charge was transformed into hatred of the only other person who knew her secret. Katy went to school on many occasions with her dress sticking to bloody welts on her back. The unending series of beatings went on month after month, year after year, until Katy finally fled from home.

She was about fifty-five when I first met her and had long since forgotten how to cry. Tears had been shut off when she was around seven. "Stop crying or I'll give you something to cry about." There was just a wistful yearning "to be people," as she put it. At first I wasn't sure what she meant. Gradually it dawned on me that all of her life she had felt inferior to other people. She even felt unworthy, I discovered, to shake hands with people or to touch them. That accounted for her unwillingness to shake hands with me on her first visit.

Katy and I had a few counseling sessions, and eventually I put her in a Yokefellow group of which I was the leader. She displayed a mixture of fear and envy as she saw group members touching one another. The first night, when the group ended in a loving circle, arms about each other, she was nearly paralyzed with fright. How desperately she longed to feel accepted, wanted, touched, held. She had never in her entire life known the meaning of love or affection. Now it was being offered, and she didn't know how to accept it. She felt clumsy and worthless.

Within a month or two Katy admitted that she enjoyed being a part of the tight circle when the session closed, arms about each other. There were a few frightening times as she allowed herself to be pushed ever so gently toward closer and warmer relationships. On one occasion I had her fantasize, eyes closed, going through the rooms of a big old house, while I played a recording of a heavy Wagnerian number. She reexperienced some

42

of her ancient childhood terror when she was not allowed to talk to anyone or to play with other children. She relived the experience of seeing another dead body found in the basement, of having her mother explain the meaning of death by showing her a dead bird with worms crawling over it. Though the events were in the past, *the hurts were in Katy,* in the present; and as she relived them, she began to become a whole person—warm, outgoing, and happy. It was—and is—a wonderful testimony to the healing power of a loving, accepting group and to the effectiveness of a "reliving experience," so that the ghosts of the past could be laid to rest.

Emotional Scar Tissue

To some extent every hurtful experience we have ever suffered has left emotional scar tissue. Each instance of real or imagined rejection and every childhood hurt in which people were involved left some major or minor scar which affects our lives in the present. We relate to persons today on the basis of how we perceived people when we were children. Either they were big, powerful, and rejecting, or big, powerful, and accepting, or a mixture of the two. Alternating currents of love and rejection can produce feelings ranging from abnormal timidity to excessive aggressiveness or even paranoia. No one can predict with certainty what the specific results of any given relationship will be.

I have already said that as a child I was afraid of people. It wasn't that I felt they would harm me; I was just unable to express myself around adults. Sometimes it wasn't too easy with my own peer group. I am unable to account for this excessive timidity, and it doesn't particularly matter. What does matter is that it took me a long time to recondition a conditioned response—to learn that it was all right to have a warm relationship with people.

How does one learn to relate openly with people? How does one go about reconditioning a conditioned response? The answer is fairly simple although doing it requires some continuity and effort. William James and a co-worker named Lange gave us what is called the James-Lange theory: "If you check or change the expression of an emotion, you thereby check or change the emotion itself." Simplified, it can be stated this way: "Do the thing you fear to do, and do it repeatedly until the fear eventually diminishes. Feelings follow action." It worked for me in a number of areas.

I had two rather determined, loving, older sisters. Both were school teachers with whom I lived for several years, and they were quietly determined that I should become a public speaker. Accordingly they had me go out for the debating team. It was the last thing I wanted to do, but debate I did. frightened half out of my mind. However, the fear began to diminish gradually. Then to my horror they had me sign up for the school play. Each year the senior class put on a play. One of my sisters was in charge; so I was given a part in each of the productions. I was a frozen-faced, emotionally rigid, and very frightened member of the cast for several years. I don't recall just why I didn't rebel. Somewhere along the way I had learned, apparently, to comply. And in the process, being on stage or talking to people became less and less frightening.

It should be added, however, that residual traces of the old reluctance to communicate still persist. I travel a great deal, and no stranger seated next to me on a plane has yet to hear me open a conversation. For one thing, I refuse to engage in casual small talk. I learned to engage in other kinds of communication, but I find myself lacking in enthusiasm for discussing minutiae, and I may add I am quite happy to have it that way.

Sources of Timidity

Timidity, shyness, fear of speaking, and fear of people all grow out of experiences or situations in early childhood. In some instances a child catches it by osmosis from a parent who is excessively passive or retiring or who may have a sense of inferiority. In other instances a child is criticized or laughed at. Inwardly he resolves never to open up again and may keep his vow. Some children who experience rejection or merely an absence of love grow up with a vague feeling that "people hurt." They learn to avoid human contact as much as possible.

The process by which an otherwise spontaneous, outgoing child learns to fear people is shown in the following:

As a child I learn that people:

reject me
hurt me
punish me
get impatient with me
lecture me
yell at me
deceive me
discipline me
won't listen to me
blame me

A door slams somewhere inside. An inner voice says:

I don't need your love
I won't trust love or big people
I won't ask for love
Love hurts

Barriers are erected:

I am afraid
I withdraw
I am inferior
I become aggressive and hostile
I become critical

I search for someone to meet my needs:

a close friend, a husband/wife, a substitute parent

Failing that, I seek substitutes such as:

money
security
attainment
recognition
honors
titles
degrees
badges
diplomas
certificates

Or I may develop a physical or emotional symptom in an unconscious effort to get love in the form of sympathy. If things go too badly, I may give up, abandon the struggle, and simply become an observer of life.

Resolving Childhood Hang-ups

In adult life we attempt to work out the hang-ups of childhood. Some succeed, others do not. Half of the hospital beds in the United States are filled with people who for one reason or another did not receive enough emotional equipment to enable them to function normally in society. The stresses are too great, and emotional illness overcomes them.

The fear of people tends to manifest itself in an avoidance of close, warm relationships. Stella is an illustration of a fairly common type. At twenty-eight she was a very unhappy, somewhat withdrawn, though pleasant young woman. She had frequent dates, but as soon as a young man became serious about marriage, she lost all interest and invariably found a way to terminate the relationship. In counseling sessions I explored her background and found about what might have been expected. Her mother was a bland, martyred, unemotional woman totally incapable of expressing warmth or love. She was very insecure and of course could not give any security to her children. The father was somewhat more outgoing, but belligerent and domineering. Stella had no memory of ever being held by either parent.

People frightened her. She said, "I never know what to say. Even with my own peer group I usually don't participate in the conversation; I feel left out." In a sense it was not just people who terrified Stella; she was afair of her own emotions. She had a deep-seated fear of anger, love, and sex and greatly feared the prospect of marriage. "If marriage is anything like what my parents had, I don't want it," she said. While that was true enough and had real validity, what she really feared was the emotions evoked by any close relationship. Fear of people is fundamentally a fear of one's own emotions.

Stella's fears were so deep-seated that she could not function well in a group experience which I had encouraged. She gave it a good try for a year and then asked, "Could you let me off the hook? I just sit there silent and petrified." Since talk therapy is usually fruitless when there is such a deeply rooted fear, we next tried something more intensive. I encouraged her to read a book or two dealing with a type of therapy that has been called by various names—primal therapy, indepth therapy, healing of memories, and other terms.

I described some of the various approaches used with this method, but Stella was certain she could never respond. However, I asked her to try it just once. To her complete surprise, and mine, she responded remarkably well for a period of about five minutes. Then the ancient fears gained control, and her response was shut off for the moment. However, she had demonstrated that she was able to let out some long-repressed, fundamental emotions. Anger, loneliness, and fear were the feelings which she expressed with great intensity during her first session. Now we knew that she was not totally blocked. In subsequent sessions Stella discovered that she did have feelings and could express them. She was not an unfeeling blob of protoplasm as she had thought. Subsequently she made great progress with in-depth therapy. Six months later Stella was engaged and had set a date for the wedding.

We Are Many-faceted Persons

It is of tremendous importance that one become aware of his feelings, be able to identify them, and accept them as part of his personality. In the case of fear of people—or any other fear for that matter—it is important to recognize that it is not true that "*I* am afraid." The totality of one's personality is not frightened. It would be more valid to say, "I am aware of the emotion of fear." Some part of the personality is experiencing fear, not all of it. To think of the entire self as being afraid, or guilty, or inferior, or hostile is a great fallacy. There is, in fact, no such thing as a single *I*, a unified self, but rather a changing community of selves. There is the noble self with integrity and morality and the weaker self which under sufficient pressure caves in and yields to temptation. There is the angry, hostile self; the loving self; the compassionate self; the punitive, mean, ingratiating, malicious selves. Any one of these may be in the ascendancy at any given time, depending upon circumstances.

In addition to these various selves there is an observer self which, either at the time or subsequently, can see and observe various members of the community of selves in operation. At times, these warped, immature, malicious selves gain control; the observer self perceives them as being less than ideal and may label the entire self as worthless and guilty. This is simply not true.

Or to employ Freudian terms, the id (the primitive self) may be in control during some given episode. Excessive anger (or some other emotion) may be expressed out of all proportion to the stimulus. The ego (the observer self or adult state) perceives this outburst as being inappropriate. The superego, loosely defined as conscience, provides the information that mother or father or society or God would not approve of such conduct. Sentence is pronounced by superego: "That's bad, wrong, sinful. You are guilty. You deserve to be punished." (The voice of the superego is the voice of parents and society but may be distorted in sundry ways.)

I am not a single entity but a multiplicity of selves, capable of unsuspected aberrations. The Apostle Paul resolved this problem to his own satisfaction when he recognized the duality of his nature. "It is no longer that I do it, but sin which dwells within me" (Rom. 7:17 RSV).

To condemn oneself for lapses is not only inappropriate and foolish, it is actually very destructive. It is not the total *I* who is stupid, sinful, weak; it is some fragment of my personality. Nor for that matter is it the total *I* that gives to the poor, shows compassion, expresses love, and aspires to the heights. That part of the self must live with the damaged selves whose conduct often astounds me.

The Origin of Our Fear of People

A basic, underlying fear of people accounts for racial prejudice. Desmond Morris describes the development of such a fear:

1. Look at the green-haired man hitting a child.
2. That green-haired man is vicious.
3. All green-haired men are vicious.
4. Green-haired men will attack anyone.
5. There's another green-haired man—hit him before he hits you. (The green-haired man, who has done nothing to provoke aggression, hits back to defend himself.)

6. There you are—that proves it: green-haired men *are* vicious.
7. Hit all green-haired men.[1]

"After the green-haired men have been hit for no reason for long enough, they do, rather naturally, become vicious. The original false prophecy has fulfilled itself and become a true prophecy.

"This is the simple story of how the out-group becomes a hated entity."[2]

In a Moscow hotel, presumably first class, I was served for breakfast cold potatoes, yoghurt, and a small piece of rather cold fish. Coffee, which came forty minutes after I had started eating, seemed to consist mainly of chickory. Since breakfast is my most important meal, I grumbled throughout the meal. (My wife said, "Well, if you can't have a good breakfast, you can always have a good grumble.") I dwelt on that atrocious breakfast throughout the day.

In the hotel lobby only American dollars were accepted for an assortment of caviar, fur caps, and needlework. The clerks refused to look at me when I asked for stamps, threw my change at me in a surly fashion, and in general conveyed the distinct impression that they disliked all Americans. In Leningrad the atmosphere was more Western, but I perceived a definite sense of paranoia from the Moscovites. (Some friends did not gain this same impression.)

In thinking about it later, I realized that the hotel staff and I were afraid of each other. Isolated from the outside world for so many years, the Russians in Moscow did seem rather paranoid. I, who had been stopped rather brusquely by four policemen for taking pictures, was also wary. We were all suspicious of each other. Their breakfast menu was "different" from what I was accustomed to. The hotel sales persons who irritated me with their sullen behavior were unfamiliar with Westerners and undoubtedly inexperienced in sales work. I learned later from our Intourist guide that they expected us to look down on them. Consequently, out of our fear of valid differences among people, we came to fear each other. It is out of such fear that hostility grows and wars erupt. I realized later than when I had met individual Russians in their homes, or in a church service, they appeared much more warm and "normal" —more like me.

Stage fright is based upon what appears to be a fear of people, but which is, at a deeper level, fear of rejection, criticism, and failure. A three- or four-year-old child can walk out on a stage unself-consciously and wave to mother and father in the audience. The child has not yet learned the possibilities of rejection and usually does not suffer from stage fright. It is only later that we learn from experience that others may judge us. So out of our fear of rejection and failure come self-doubt, fear of people, and consequently a fear of close, warm relationships. Then we settle for the banal in conversation, dealing in trivialities instead of getting to know each other at a deep level. We fear being known lest we expose ourselves to ridicule or censure.

Out of fear of rejection and criticism many husbands and wives spend their lives discussing only minutiae. Strangely enough many couples are able to learn how to communicate better in a properly led sharing group than at home. I was conducting a demonstration Yoke-fellow group of about ten persons with seventy-five observers looking on. The group members were given the ground rules: be personal, share feelings only, no attack or criticism, but reserve the right to express your own needs and feelings. One very thoughtful man in the small group looked at his wife and said, "You know, we've been married twelve years, and I don't think I've ever told you that I feel shot down when you criticize me in public."

His wife looked aghast and replied, "John, I never knew you felt that way. I always thought of my comments as whimsical little jokes. I didn't realize you felt attacked. Why haven't you told me before?"

"Well," her husband said, "you always argue every point and get defensive, and I never win an argument. I don't want to argue about it, but I just want to let you know how I feel when you tell some of your supposedly hilarious stories in public, always at my expense."

His wife looked thoughtful. "Yes, I see what you mean. I wish you'd told me before, but I guess I am defensive because I don't like to be criticized. I'm grateful for this group experience, so you could feel free to tell me."

"Yeah," he said, "and I suppose I'd have to admit to being chicken because I haven't wanted to get embroiled in a lengthy argument at home. I feel safer here."

"I'm glad," she said.

Chapter 4

FEAR OF EMOTIONS

> *To give up our pretensions is as blessed a relief as to have them gratified.*
>
> WILLIAM JAMES

In common with most people I can make little sense out of some of my dreams, but I had two frightening ones, quite close together, which were almost self-explanatory. In the first dream I was standing in an open space, facing a vague, indistinct figure whose face I could not see. He walked toward me, and though I had no idea what threat he posed, I was deathly afraid of him. He made no threatening gesture, but I backed away in mortal fear. Finally I saw that I was just outside an open gate. Instantly I seized the gate, slammed it shut, dropped down a convenient manhole in the pavement, and pulled the metal cover over my head.

I awoke feeling very frightened but with no idea of what I was afraid. Gradually it dawned on me. I had dived down a manhole into the depths below. The *depths* would symbolize the unconscious mind. It was *sub*, under the conscious. But who was the threatening man? What did he symbolize? I put the matter away, hoping that I might get further insight. A few nights later I had a companion dream which shed some light.

In the dream I thought I was awake. I was certain that I had my eyes open. Standing beside the bed looking at me was a dark, threatening man. He just stood there silently. I didn't know what he intended doing. He did nothing, actually, except to stand there. I was terrified. I thought of getting up to grapple with him but felt immobilized. Some portion of my mind forced me to take some action, so I opened my eyes. No one was there, of course. Now who was he? I lay awake a long time trying to discover his identity. Then I got a clue. Both he and the man in the previous dream were the same person: myself or another part of me. They represented the four-fifths of the personality which consists of emotions. I knew intellectually that I had a certain fear of some of my deeper emotions, but I had no idea it was *that* great! Perhaps I had better do something about it. I had no desire to go through life partially paralyzed by an inordinate fear of my feelings.

The first step was to discover what emotions I was most afraid of. This took a bit of soul-searching. Eventually I came to the conclusion that, in common with many people, I had a great fear of my anger and of my sensual-sexual self. In my childhood the words *sensual* and *sexual,* which sound somewhat alike, became virtually synonymous. The word *sex* was never mentioned in our home. Nor was it ever mentioned in church or school, but the terrible results of unbridled sensuality and of certain unnamed excesses were darkly hinted at from the pulpit.

It was all very confusing. The Bible we studied in Sunday school seemed to be a very sexual book, at least in spots. The Song of Solomon sounded to me very much like a beautiful love poem, but I had been assured that it was an allegory of God's love for Israel. Other authorities were equally insistent that it depicted the love of Christ for his bride, the church. This was taught in one of the seminaries I attended. No one seemed to have the honesty or courage to say that there was no internal evidence that this was so and that the work appeared to express the beauty of a lovely and passionate love affair. This very tender and explicit love poem at the very least seems to sanctify the physical, spiritual, and emotional aspects of human love. And why, indeed, should God not place his seal of approval upon romantic love, upon human passion, upon the divinely ordained attraction of the sexes? But in my childhood this would have been a terrible thing to say. It was as though there was a conspiracy of silence about human sexuality. There were some things decent people just didn't talk about. If today's culture has gone to the other extreme and cast off all restraints, this is simply another illustration of the fact that too much of anything can be disastrous.

All Human Emotions Are Valid

In San Francisco, near where I live, resides a man named Anton LaVey, the leader of the Satanic Church. He says, "We hold Satan to be the symbolic personal savior who takes care of mundane, fleshly carnal things. God exists as a universal force, a balancing force in nature too impersonal to care one whit whether we live or die. Jesus takes care of the spiritual aspect, but the devil takes care of the carnal side of man."

That type of theology is reminiscent of the religious atmosphere in which I grew up. In those distant days no one would have ascribed to God any interest in the purely physical aspect of life. While it was never stated as explicitly as Anton LaVey has put it, one gained the impression that God dealt with the spirit but that all which was "of the flesh" was of the devil.

Consequently millions of people grew up in a culture which denied the senses or at least repudiated sensuality. It took me a long while to come to terms at a feeling level with the idea that all human emotions are valid. Though our culture today is far less life-denying, there are still numberless people who are terribly afraid of their emotions. For instance, I learned at the age of four that anger was forbidden. Until then, I was told later, I had been fairly free in my expression of all human emotions. At the end of a large stick I learned that if I wanted to survive I would have to be totally compliant and never express anger. Outwardly I complied. Inwardly I was still rebellious, biding my time, waiting to get my own way. I became a submarine. If I could not express negative emotions openly, I could get my way by subterfuge, using whatever devious methods seemed necessary to achieve my goals. This, of course, leaves something to be desired. For one thing it was not honest. But it was safe.

A friend of mine related an incident which illustrates a difficulty encountered by people who cannot express negative emotions. He and his wife had been married for sixteen years. Every Thanksgiving during those years they had driven some eight hundred miles so that they could spend the holidays with her parents. He had no particular desire to drive sixteen hundred miles round trip on icy roads to visit her family, but it seemed to give her so much pleasure that he manfully put up with the annual ordeal. Finally on his was home after his sixteenth trip he said, "Honey, I know how much this annual visit to your parents means to you, but to be honest I am getting to resent it just a little. I wonder if we could settle for every other year."

She interrupted: "You mean you've been doing this all these years just for *me*? Good grief, I've hated it! But *you* seemed to derive so much enjoyment that I went along with it. I thought you got a real kick out of it."

"I faked it," he said. They both laughed and then sat in silence for some miles as they considered how much better it would have been if they had been able to communicate their honest feelings.

This is not to suggest that complete honesty is always a great virtue. A tactful reticence is sometimes an important ingredient in a good marriage. To express all of our feelings consistently would be disastrous in most relationships, but there are times when a wise expression of genuine feelings can be very helpful.

In a counseling session, a man told me that he had developed the habit of retreating from both his wife's criticism and her anger. This made her all the more furious, and she demanded that he stand up and fight things out. On his part he had a morbid fear of an angry confrontation, a holdover from childhood experiences. His wife kept insisting it was weak of him to retreat whenever there was an argument. One day when she had said something rather sharp to him, he said he could feel the temptation to retreat, but instead he turned and said, "All right, you want me to stand up and slug it out with you toe to toe. I'll do it. Whenever you talk to me as if I were one of the children, I become furiously angry, and if you ever do it again, I'm going to let you have it."

She started to flare up, and he said, "If you get angry now and want to argue, all I've got to say is that I've had my say and I have nothing more to tell you."

She closed her mouth and then asked in a quieter tone, "Are you saying that I speak to you in the same tone of voice as I do the children?"

He replied, "Yes, you yell at them, and then you use the same tone of voice with me, and I refuse to be one of the children." He said that he felt good about his ability finally to express his true feelings. He also added that his wife never again used the same tone of voice in talking to him as she did with the children. He had been reacting in fear of his hostility and had retreated, but when challenged by his wife to stand up and talk about it, he transformed his fear into courage and finally faced the situation.

The fear of expressing negative feelings seems to spring out of a sincere concern for the welfare of the other person, and to some extent this may be true. But at a deeper level, some of our reluctance to share honest feelings is the fear of rejection. Where this is a factor, it is usually learned early in childhood. The child may learn that in order to survive and maintain his position in the home it is better to become compliant. He discovers that he can get more love by being always agreeable and compliant.

Fear of Our Basic Emotions

Gregory was just such a child. He was very sickly during the first four years of life, and most of his mother's time was devoted to caring for him. He became an excessively compliant little boy, deeply resented by his brother and sisters because he seemed to be getting more love than they. He was forty, unmarried, and an emotional cripple when I first saw him. A long series of counseling sessions followed.

Gregory's symptoms were manifold. He was phobic, obsessive-compulsive, and devoted most of every day to a ritualistic routine of hand-washing, checking, and rechecking everything he did. He took a leave of absence for a year simply because he did not have enough psychic energy to hold a job and carry out his numberless rituals. He had already had a great deal of therapy. Both shock therapy and a prefrontal lobotomy had been proposed. These were desperate, last-minute measures, indicative of the severity of his problem. Gregory rejected both.

I wish I could say that Gregory experienced a permanent cure. Actually he did get much better for several years. As the result of what I term "paradoxical intention" therapy (see chap. 12, "Reconditioning the Conditioned Response"), he improved remarkably and was able to return to work. I had told him that he might need some years of continued private and group therapy if he was to maintain his emotional well-being, but he said, "I feel much more like a real person than before I got sick," and abandoned the means by which he had been rescued from mental illness. Two years or so later Gregory experienced a relapse. This time the symptoms were more severe, and several years of intensified therapy of various types were insufficient to help him regain the lost ground. Discussing his case with a psychiatrist friend, I asked, "Have you ever experienced cases like this where there is a remission of symptoms, followed by a relapse, with greater difficulty in getting the patient back to normal?"

"Yes," he replied, "and I don't fully understand why. It's a commonplace experience here in our clinic."

But back to Gregory. It developed that he still had a great emotional dependence upon his mother. He lived at home, and his mother expressed the same tender devotion as when he was a sickly child. He had never expressed anger toward her, even when he felt deeply resentful of her loving dominance. For that matter, he could not remember ever expressing anger to anyone. He was a totally compliant individual, incapable of expressing any deep feelings. This carried over into his other relationships. Though he had dated a few times, he had never formed any but the most temporary relationships with either men or women.

Here was a man whose whole emotional life had been stunted. Unable to express either deep positive or negative emotions, he was crippled. In order to keep the repressed emotions of anger and sex under control, he displaced those forbidden emotions onto phobias, some of which were terrifying. His daily rituals of ceaseless hand-washing, bathing, and checking prevented some of the forbidden feelings from surfacing. As long as he devoted most of his time and energy to his rituals, there was less opportunity for the unacceptable emotions of anger and sex to reach consciousness.

In the New Testament there is a reference to people who are initially converted and then fall by the wayside. After which, the author of Hebrews says, "It is impossible to restore [them] again" (see Heb. 6:4 RSV). The principle would seem to carry over to those who, having achieved some form of liberation from emotional illness, give up "the means of grace" and then discover too late that it seems almost impossible to get back to

59

the same "state of grace" they had reached previously. My own conclusions, based on a number of such experiences and the observation of the author of Hebrews, is that one who has worked his way out of spiritual and emotional distress would do well not to abandon the steps by which he achieved wholeness. It is gratifying to be able to report that Gregory, at forty-six, has fully recovered.

Incongruent Feelings

One of many factors which result in a denial of emotions is an environment in which parents feel one way but act another. A child growing up in such a family sees his parents smiling sweetly, hears the dulcet tones, but is aware at the same time that they are hostile. The younger the child, the more readily the deceit is perceived. This provides the child with an inconsistent emotional climate in which to grow up, and he becomes confused.

Another factor is the parental message, spoken or implied: "I am entitled to get angry, but you are not. I am justified in my anger, but it is never permissible for you to express negative emotions." Then the message may become more complex: "Don't hold your anger in. Express it. Don't be sullen. We don't stand for that. Let it out. It's good for you." But the next time his honest anger is expressed may not be the appropriate time, so far as the parents are concerned, and he is rebuked for having a nasty disposition. He is put in a double bind and unconsciously decides either to become compliant, so as not to lose parental love, or to displace the anger and act out his aggression in ways which are satisfying but which if discovered may get him into trouble.

A woman married to a complacent, uncommunicative husband got hold of a book titled *The Intimate Enemy*.[1] She asked her husband to read it, but he never got around to it. Eventually she decided to read some pertinent passages to him. In the middle of the third page she heard deep, regular breathing and looked up.

He was sound asleep. "I wanted to kill him," she said. His going to sleep was an unconscious defense mechanism, the way he had handled his parents with whom he could not communicate. Later, she reported, he picked up the book and read it through. Eventually, since he recognized a definite problem in the area, they did make progress in opening up the channels of communication.

The Denial of Emotions

Morris was about eight or nine when his father died. His mother had been an emotionally rigid, unresponsive person, and the father had never been able to express feelings. Morris learned to bury his emotions too. He recalled walking to school whistling after being told that his father had died during the night. He was about forty-three when this memory surfaced and he dealt with it in a group experience. We wondered how a child of nine could so easily bury all feelings. In time, through his Yokefellow group and some private counseling, he got in touch with his emotions and learned that he did not have to repress them. In the process he became a much more effective personality.

A woman of sixty-five shared in a counseling session an insight she had gotten the day before. A high government official under fire had not responded to charges against him. Miriam followed the developments closely on television and said that she found herself becoming unreasonably angry with the official. "Why in heaven's name doesn't he respond, defend himself, or make some comment about the charges?" she asked. Later she realized that she was reacting with unaccountable hostility. "It was a full-scale overreaction," she said. It was not he at whom she was angry, but her silent, unresponsive father. His silence, she said, left her puzzled and upset. He expressed neither anger nor love nor irritation. He was always the same, always predictable, never upset, never affectionate, a kind of bland nonperson.

Miriam's displaced anger illustrates something that

often happens in a marriage. A wife may displace onto her husband some ancient frustrations which really stem from her relationship with her father; or a husband may react with irritation or anger toward his wife when it is really an unresolved problem with his mother that is the difficulty. I have heard many mothers admit that the anger expressed toward their children is often leftover hostility which they could not readily express toward their husbands either because the husband had departed or because it was safer to scream at a small child than to attack the husband verbally.

When Emotions Are Repressed

Elise joined a Yokefellow group when she was in her sixties. She had an excessively flat, monotonous voice totally devoid of inflection. Someone asked her if she were depressed, after referring to her flat voice. She denied being depressed, but later admitted that she probably suffered from a generalized depression of long-standing. The group helped her feel her way gradually back into her childhood, where, they sensed, her lack of emotional response had originated. Thoughtfully she reported: "I can hear my father now: 'Be still, don't make so much noise, don't bother me, quiet down.' It's about the only memory I have of him. There was no praise, no approval, no affection, just an irritable insistence that I be quiet. I suppose I leveled off my voice as I leveled off my personality, so it would be flat and inoffensive. I must prefer the predictable to the spontaneous because I never do anything spontaneously. I lead a gray, monotonous kind of life, with no ups and no downs, just like you say my voice is. Mother was always depressed, and perhaps I picked up some of her depression by osmosis. Maybe I've always been depressed and wouldn't know what it was like to be otherwise."

In the group, various activities were programed to enable the members to get in touch with their feelings. In Elise's case, she was encouraged, with several other inhibited members, to undertake some things which required spontaneity. At first it was mildly threatening to her, but she tried and gradually began to experience a sense of release as she expressed the whole spectrum of emotions—anger, love, warmth, joy. It was the first time in a long life that she had been encouraged or permitted to express anything but "safe" emotions. It was a joy to see her erupt with anger at an inert object but actually expressing the hostility she still had toward her unresponsive father, and then to express warmth and affection for members of the group—a difficult task at first, but a skill she was determined to acquire.

Studies have shown that at the age of five nearly all children measure high on creativity, imagination, and spontaneity. By age seven only 10 percent of the same children score high on creativity. Among adults, only 2 percent rate high on creativity, imagination, and spontaneity. The conclusion of researchers is that these emotional responses have been stifled by criticism and fear of failure induced by rejecting adults. Some of it, of course, is the result of unconscious imitation of adults who pass on to children their emotionally starved personalities. Some of it appears to be the result of an archaic educational system. How sad that creativity, imagination, and spontaneity should be stifled by a home and school environment, producing emotionally unresponsive robots programed to react in a carefully predictable, bland, noncreative way.

In this connection, Carl Gustav Jung contended that Western culture has overemphasized the masculine ideals of rationality, abstract thinking, and ego control. He felt that the feminine values of intuition and emotional response have been very dangerously repressed, robbing man of his soul and woman of her individuality.

Displaced Anger and Projection

Gary provides an excellent illustration of displaced anger. He had served time in prison, and when he was eligible for parole, I had secured a position for him. He proved to have an excellent mind, and I helped raise some money to enable him to undertake postgraduate work. He was doing well in school, but he was unusually dependent upon me. I resolved to try to get him to accept, gradually, some responsibility for his own future. This was creating considerable anxiety on his part, but I was gently pushing him very slowly toward the goal of greater independence. In one Yokefellow group session, Gary, who never expressed anger, suddenly erupted. Turning to me, with his voice shaking, and very red in the face, he shouted: "I've been watching you. I know what your game is. You try to get everyone around you dependent upon you. Then you manipulate them. That's a terrible thing to do, and you're not going to do it for me." He went on in that vein for some time.

When his verbal attack was over, I said, in effect, "If the group perceives any validity to this, I'd be glad to know it. Often we humans are blind to our own motives and actions, but, Gary, I'd like to point out some things. You have said that you were never able to express anger toward your father, who was seldom around. He was not really a father to you. You had no one to rebel against in adolescence because by that time you were spending most of your time burglarizing houses. Granted, it was an unconscious effort to take something of value as a substitute for the love you couldn't get at home, so there is no judgment involved.

"Now you've made me your father. I'm trying to help you gradually toward more independence, and you're rebelling against me, the substitute father, and against the idea of being pushed out of the nest. You really would like to go on being dependent on me as you've often demonstrated. You're actually projecting onto me your own desire to be dependent. I don't want to control you. But it's O.K. to blow up at me, to shout at me, to be as angry as you want—now or in the future."

Later Gary was able to see the validity of this, though

for a week or two he had difficulty in understanding it. For one thing he had never been that angry before and wondered why. He was glad that there was at least one person he could shout at and get away with it. It was a creative experience, for he had needed to express his anger at his father, in this case at the substitute father, and discover that the roof did not fall in. All humans experience the emotion of anger. Even David, "a man after God's own heart," explodes with violent anger in some of the psalms. Anger is as basic an emotion as love and hunger and fear.

The Child Who Is Seldom Angry

If a child expresses anger, the parents may say, "Go to your room until you can be nice." Such an approach provides the emotional climate for enormous anxiety, which may express itself later either in the form of depression or in physical symptoms ranging from migraine headaches, asthma, and neurodermatitis, to rheumatoid arthritis, ulcers, or coronaries. Many such children are hyperkinetic. The child who wins acceptance and approval for never being angry may grow into an adult who is totally unaware of his anger. His approach to life may range from saccharine sweetness to a bland, stoical indifference to all emotions. The only clue to his unconscious conflict may be a deep depression, a dampening of all emotions, or some physical symptoms.

We handle our anger in at least six basic ways: (1) retreat in fear, (2) placate with smiling compliance, (3) confront the situation with controlled rage, (4) attack with hostility, (5) explode in uncontrolled, panicky fury, or (6) freeze. We tend to react to anger-producing situations on the basis of "parent tapes"—the way we were conditioned as children. According to Dr. Karl Menninger, the child begins his life in anger.

Reexperiencing Birth

My own observation and experiments tend to confirm Dr. Menninger's observation. My son happens to be an excellent subject for hypnosis. He had learned self-hypnosis and would take himself down as far as he could go. Upon receiving a finger signal from him, I would take him still further.

On one occasion, in a purely experimental mood, we agreed that we would undertake to have him reexperience birth. I took him back to the very moment of birth and left him there. When I brought him out of the hypnotic trance, he grinned and said, "I was angry and scared when I was born. For one thing, somebody was beating on me, and the whole experience was so new and foreign to anything I'd known in the warmth and safety of the womb that I was half scared out of my mind." He had not "remembered" but actually relived the entire experience of birth in considerable detail.

Although the literature concerning hypnosis contains many similar references to reliving the birth trauma, I wanted to determine for myself whether my son was unconsciously indulging in fantasy or experiencing reality. Consequently, I undertook the same experiment with the young wife of an associate. She, too, was a good subject and readily went back to the moment of birth. Her first comment was that it was terribly, frighteningly bright. She was cold and scared, she said.

I neither affirm nor deny the validity of their feelings but simply report them for what they are worth. In both instances the two subjects under hypnosis experienced intense fear at the moment of birth. On the basis of pure logic it seems valid to assume that an infant, after peaceful months in the warmth of the womb, would be aware of pain, shock, fear, and anger as the result of the forcible ejection from that comfortable home and being plunged into a radically different world with blazing lights, confusing noises, and, as the crowning indignity, being held upside down by the legs and spanked.

Infants seem to begin their lives in a state of vague, diffused excitement. There is a considerable body of evidence that anxiety exists before birth. One to three months before birth an infant may have an accelerated heartbeat if there is a sudden noise nearby. The heartbeat of the infant is increased at birth, evidence of increased anxiety. Upon recovering from the birth trauma the infant usually begins to experience and express emotions of either distress or pleasure, depending upon how secure and comfortable he feels. Authorities disagree on how early specific emotions such as fear and anger are expressed. Some feel that it is not before the age of six months. Others are confident that fear and anger are being felt and expressed as early as the first few days of life.

Before a child is a year old he may be manifesting a budding sense of humor and at times sheer pleasure, particularly in response to a parent who is playing with him. By this age he may also seem to express affection, a prelude to the emotion of love.

By the second year he is able to express sorrow, hostility, anxiety, and fear. Through the third year he experiences and expresses a broader range of emotions. But by the age of five he has already learned to disguise his emotions, to pretend emotions he does not feel, in order to avoid punishment or to win parental approval. By the age of seven a good 70 percent of his spontaneity has been lost, due in part to imitating parents and other authorities and partly because he has been punished for revealing feelings which make adults uncomfortable.

By the time he is an adult at least 90 percent of his original spontaneity and creativity has been lost. By wearing a mask he generates considerable anxiety, for it is a genuine burden to pretend what he is not. He may be spending from fifty to seventy percent of his psychic energy in maintaining the mask required by society. Depending upon various factors, the child is already—at age six or seven—a potential victim of an anxiety neurosis.

Many psychiatrists believe that birth is the most traumatic event that ever occurs in the life of a typical individual. One outstanding psychiatrist traces all neuroses back to the birth trauma. With this in mind, Dr. Frederick Leboyer, a French obstetrician, has written a book, *Birth Without Violence*,[2] in which he outlines a remarkable new technique which, he claims, makes healthier infants and less neurotic adults. He maintains that birth is the most serious trauma anyone is likely to experience. The trauma is intensified, he says, by present-day birth techniques—glaring delivery room lights, the noise, the shaking of the infant to start breathing, the instantaneous cutting of the umbilical cord, the drops in the eyes, and the sudden cleaning of ears and mouth.

Dr. Frederick Leboyer says, "I had participated in the birth of over seven thousand babies before I realized that the first cry that everyone is so pleased to hear is actually a frightful scream of terror. Hell does not come at the end of life but at the very beginning. The newborn comes into a strange new environment after what for him has been an agonizing struggle. He leaves a world of warmth and silence and darkness and enters one of coolness and clamor and light. No wonder he screams! And we are so alienated from nature that we smile and take the scream as a sign of health."

Dr. Leboyer's radically different method of delivery is disarmingly simple and so obvious one wonders why it has not been practiced before. He eliminates the factors which he sees as upsetting to the infant. Births take place under strictly controlled conditions, with the intent of assuring the serenity of the newborn infant. When the infant's head becomes visible the overhead lights are instantly dimmed, and physician and nurses speak in whispers. The baby is then taken very slowly and with great care. When he emerges, the infant is placed on his mother's abdomen. While resting there, he is stroked gently by the nurses. In a few moments the baby, on his back, begins to stretch, unfolds his limbs "like a flower opening to the sun."

After the infant has begun to breathe normally, usually about ten minutes after birth, the physician cuts the umbilical cord and places the child in lukewarm water. This provides an environment similar to the one from which he has just emerged. Leboyer insists that the newborn child, when no more than fifteen minutes old, actually appears to smile with pleasure in the bath. In a filmed birth the baby did not cry once during the entire process.

"Birth without terror" is the term applied to this process. Although numerous American obstetricians reacted with skepticism to the published report of the new birth process, it seems quite likely that in time the Leboyer technique will be the accepted way of childbirth in our society.[8] The tremendous potential of the new concept is underscored by one of several thousand letters from grateful mothers. A mother whose daughter was born this way some years ago wrote: "The baby you delivered is not like my other children. She is much more serene and much calmer. She is gay, relaxed. She never seems scared of life."

Many psychiatrists agree that perhaps some of our aggressive impulses originate in the trauma and terror of birth. If this is true, we need not feel responsible for and guilty about the neurotic behavior patterns which mar our lives and relationships. Our sole responsibility then becomes that of beginning, at this point, to do the best we can under the circumstances. We cannot alter the past; we are responsible only for what we do with the future.

Chapter 5

FEAR OF THE FUTURE

> *It has been well said that no man ever sank under the burden of the day. It is when tomorrow's burden is added to the burden of today that the weight is more than a man can bear. Never load yourselves so, my friends. If you find yourselves so loaded, at least remember this; it is your own doing, not God's. He begs you leave the future to him, and mind the present.*
>
> GEORGE MACDONALD

I was up at two A.M. this morning and never went back to sleep," said the woman on my right. "I never sleep well when I'm facing a change." She had no idea that she harbored a mild floating anxiety. She was a highly intelligent, delightful woman. She, her husband, and my wife and I ate together on an ocean cruise. Like millions of otherwise well-integrated people she managed her life well, functioned above the average in society, and was a very creative person.

The reason for the sleeplessness was that we were nearing the home port. Though this certainly was no cause for conscious anxiety, she was tense enough so that at two A.M. she was wide awake. A floating anxiety can attach itself to almost anything—a decision that needs to be made, a new or strange situation, facing familiar situations which nevertheless have negative associations. The fundamental anxiety is seldom anything that you can put your finger on. The roots usually go far back into childhood.

Fear of the future is really a catch all term which covers a multitude of nebulous but very real anxieties. It may have originated in fear of making decisions, which manifests itself now as indecisiveness. Such a fear sometimes is caught from an indecisive parent. More often it stems from the childhood fear of making the wrong decision for which the child may be scolded or punished in some manner. The result of such treatment often causes an individual to have a vague, unreasoning fear of penalties for making a mistake.

A Yokefellow group was taking one of the spiritual growth inventories provided by Yokefellows, Inc., in Burlingame, California. One of the men received an evaluation slip which said, among other things, "You would have a tendency to greet any new or sudden proposal with a negative response since you need time to make up your mind." He rejected the idea immediately.

His wife interrupted: "Hold it! That explains a lot of things about you that I never understood until this minute. Any time I make a suggestion of any sort, you instantly veto it and give two or ten emphatic reasons why it isn't any good. Then an hour or a week later you come up with the same idea as though it were your own. I thought there was something radically wrong with you, but now I understand. You're a delayed reactor!"

Further discussion revealed that in childhood he had been severely criticized when he made what his parents considered a wrong decision. Consequently, in order to avoid having to make decisions, he had unconsciously developed the negative habit of vetoing all suggestions. This gave him time to consider the situation at leisure.

Indecision Can Immobilize Us

A somewhat more serious manifestation of the same problem is seen when an individual becomes virtually immobilized and cannot make any decisions at all. Midway between the two behavior patterns are those who ponder every decision, however small, weigh each possibility, and discuss it at great length. I know otherwise normal individuals for whom making a dinner selection from a menu is a monumental decision involving changes, discussion with the waiter, consultations with friends, and finally an indecisive selection which often does not prove completely satisfactory when served. Such symptoms can be irritating to others, but when indecisiveness leaves one immobilized on dead center, it becomes really serious.

Fear of the future is often a deeply rooted fear of judgment, of unfortunate consequences, of being chastised for mistakes. To one who is not troubled by such an anxiety, it seems simple enough. "Just make up your mind. Either way it won't be fatal." But it is never that simple for the indecisive person. He is saddled with an ancient fear, originating in childhood. He is seldom conscious of the fear and aware only of the great anxiety generated if he is pressured to make a quick decision.

Frank had achieved enormous success under very unusual circumstances. His education was limited but not his intelligence or drive. In a relatively small town in the Midwest he opened a small store. Through clever merchandising methods he achieved tremendous success. People came from fifty miles away to shop at his store. He enlarged the operation several times and eventually received national recognition in the field of retail merchandising. He made decisions quickly, and they usually proved to be wise. He was decisive, firm, friendly, open, and spontaneous. Then, after some years of great success, a business recession struck. Business fell off. In the belief that business conditions would soon improve, he made certain other quick decisions, most of which proved disastrous. He did not lose his business but came very close to doing so. Eventually, after taking his losses, he sold the firm to his employees and moved away.

Ancient Sources of Present Fears

I came to know Frank when he took over the business management of a denominational organization. He was a delightful person. I had a few difficulties with him which stemmed from his total inability to give a definite answer to any straightforward question. He, who had once made instant decisions, now hedged, equivocated, delayed, explained, and asked for more time and information.

On one occasion, after asking for a decision on some relatively routine matter and receiving vague and indecisive replies, I said with considerable impatience, "Frank, when you have made up your mind, call me back," and hung up. Almost immediately I felt ashamed of my impatience with this gentle and loving man, but at the same time I was exasperated by his inability to give a straight yes or no. When he called back later, he was apologetic, but we spent another ten minutes during which I said a number of times, "Frank, the answer is either yes or no. I don't much care which it is. Just pick one or the other." Eventually I pressured him into making a decision. This had happened so often in the past that I was familiar with his problem, but it was still difficult to deal with. Here was a highly intelligent man who had been traumatized by a business failure and was now virtually incapable of rendering a decision for fear of consequences.

Badges, Honors, and Degrees

A psychiatric dictionary defines *ambition* as "a defense against shame." This harmonizes with Alfred Adler's insistence that the need to compensate for our inferiority feelings is one of the strongest human drives. Virtually all cultures have developed various forms of recognition such as honors and titles. These are means by which we reassure ourselves that we have succeeded rather than failed. Achievement, wealth, titles, degrees —earned or honorary—are all status symbols which certify success in some way. Lodges, clubs, government, the academic and scientific world—in fact, organizations of all kinds—have some form of distinction or honors to award those who for one reason or another are deemed worthy to receive these status symbols. Why are they sought so avidly? These are the means by which we allay our anxiety resulting from feelings of inferiority or helplessness, of not being noticed or applauded. In short, these badges, titles, and degrees help prevent us from feeling anxiety. If one can only achieve enough titles or honors or recognition, he no longer need feel the sharp stab of failure or the dull throb of diffused anxiety based on feelings of inferiority.

This is not to deprecate the almost universal custom of rewarding achievement, but on the other hand Jesus lashed out at the Pharisees: "How can you believe, you who receive honors one from another?" (paraphrase of John 5:44). There seems implicit in his rhetorical question the idea that there is some subtle evil at the heart of an overemphasis upon honors.

Fear prepares us for fight or flight, but there is always a third option—to freeze. In some instances this can be fraught with great danger, particularly if the situation calls for flight and the person is immobolized with fear. But there are other instances when becoming immobilized can be a better solution than either fight or flight. Unfortunately when fear is strong enough to produce an instantaneous reaction, there is seldom time to give deliberate thought to the matter. One must learn over a period of time to react in a manner that will be most productive under a given set of circumstances.

Fear of the future can express itself as fear of financial insecurity. I recall a number of conversations with a widow who had worked diligently and invested wisely in order to have enough money for her old age. When I knew her, toward the end of her life, she was worth in the neighborhood of half a million dollars and lived in the basement of her home with two unmarried sisters. Each time I visited her, she bitterly denounced the tax collector. She was very agitated over the fact that a few apartments were not rented in one of her buildings. When she was close to death but still rational—or at least as much so as she had been for a number of years —she brought up the subject of her will. She said she planned to leave her money to relatives, all of whom were millionaires.

"Since they are all well-to-do," I said, "what do you think of leaving a portion of your estate to some very worthy cause?" I named a few which I thought might appeal to her. She became very upset. Curious as to how deeply ingrained her financial insecurity was and how much it had affected her mind, I pushed hard for the next half-hour. "If one day you must give an account of your life and your possessions, how will you feel about reporting that you refused to leave a dime to some very wonderful and needy causes?" She grew almost incoherent. I feared for a moment that she might have a heart attack. The anxiety had nothing to do with her approaching death, which she accepted. It was the enormous threat posed by even considering letting her money go out of the control of herself or family members. Any virtue—such as saving for one's old age—if carried to an extreme can become a vice, or in her case, a neurosis.

Fear of the future can take the form of refusing to think about it. For instance, one of America's wealthiest men, according to his biographer, refused to permit anyone to speak of death in his presence. His friends avoided the subject as the plague. The very thought of death created enormous anxiety and anger in him.

A somewhat more amorphous form of fear is experienced by many people. It manifests itself as a vague, nameless, indefinable foreboding. There is usually a fear that something dreadful is about to happen. One woman told me of her constant dread that something terrible might happen to her children. We were able to trace this irrational fear to an old, unresolved guilt feeling. Theoretically she should have been able to experience a sense of forgiveness and peace after having confessed it to God, but there are two important aspects to forgiveness not often dealt with. First, time does not diminish guilt; and second, one can often achieve a sense of release and forgiveness only after sharing the guilt problem with another.

The future must have seemed dreadfully bleak and fearful to Dietrich Bonhoeffer, in a Nazi concentration camp. All about him men were dying while others were succumbing to the deadly lassitude and stupor induced by hopelessness. Bonhoeffer wrote:

Who Am I?

Who am I? They often tell me
I stepped from my cell's confinement
calmly, cheerfully, firmly,
like a Squire from his country house.

Who am I? They often tell me
I used to speak to my warders
freely and friendly and clearly,
as though it were mine to command.

Who am I? They also tell me
I bore the days of misfortune
equably, smilingly, proudly,
like one accustomed to win.

Am I then really that which other men tell of?
Or am I only what I myself know of myself?
Restless and longing and sick, like a bird in a cage,
struggling for breath, as though hands were compressing
    my throat,

Yearning for colours, for flowers, for the voices of birds,
thirsting for words of kindness, for neighborliness,
tossing in expectation of great events,
powerlessly trembling for friends at an infinite distance,
weary and empty at praying, at thinking, at making,
faint, and ready to say farewell to it all.

Who am I? This or the Other?
Am I one person today and tomorrow another?
Am I both at once? A hypocrite before others,

and before myself a contemptible woebegone weakling?
Or is something within me still like a beaten army
fleeing in disorder from victory already achieved?

Who am I? They mock me, these lonely questions of mine.
Whoever I am, Thou knowest, O God I am thine.[1]

Man Is Not a Static Being

As Bonhoeffer implies, no one is totally this or that.
We are not completely fearful persons, nor are we alto-
gether courageous. We are a mixture. Whether we react
with fear or courage may depend upon any number of
factors: the situation, our metabolism on that particular
day, what has transpired just prior to the emergency,
and perhaps a hundred other factors. Normally timid
persons have sometimes reacted with unbelievable courage in some sudden crisis, while strong men have on
other occasions panicked and fled in terror.

The future, because it is an unknown factor, poses a
very great threat to many people. Every step into the
future is moving into the unfamiliar and therefore can
be very threatening. It can mean parting from the
familiar past and launching out into an unknown and
uncharted sea of uncertainties. Yet this is what life is
all about. It requires courage. There are no absolute
assurances of success, no guarantees of fulfillment or
even of safety.

I happen to live in the San Francisco area, very near
the San Andreas fault. Many dire predictions have been
made to the effect that part of California will one day
slide into the ocean. Seismologists have said that a
major earthquake is long overdue and that the longer
it is delayed the more severe it will be. Yet enormous
skyscrapers continue to be built in San Francisco, virtually straddling the San Andreas fault. Only time will
tell whether the builders are foolhardy, wise, or lucky.
I may awaken some dark night to find my home shaking and possibly collapsing as the long-awaited quake
announces its final arrival. I have often wondered why
people were so foolhardy as to live on or near the

slopes of Mt. Vesuvius. For all I know I am just as foolish. Yet the presence of a million and a half others in the San Francisco Bay area gives me a sense of companionship in the face of what, to most of us, is a very remote possibility of disaster.

One cannot insure against all possibilities of danger. I may well be struck down by a passing truck or a coronary long before the threatened earthquake arrives. I choose to live in the knowledge that the future is unknown, unpredictable, unsure; and whether physical death arrives next week or twenty years from now is not of transcendent importance. I confess, however, to a very human desire to prepare for most possible contingencies. So I do take some reasonable precautions—such as quake insurance on my home.

"The future is so uncertain," said a young woman of my acquaintance. She was thinking of her forthcoming marriage, and, though deeply in love, there were many questions lingering in her mind. The soaring divorce rate suggested to her the possibility that her marriage might be no more stable than the one in three which ends in divorce. (The rate is much higher than that in the area in which she lives.) She was planning to go on working to help her husband through graduate school. He planned to enter law, but his grades in college had been less than remarkable. Would he make good? Could he pass the bar exams? These and a dozen other uncertainties came to her mind; yet, with the optimism of youth, they made their plans as if failure or defeat were highly improbable.

Fear and Death

Many people are heard to say, "It is not death that I fear, but the possibility of a long, painful illness." Here again is one of life's great uncertainties. Some fortunate individuals die peacefully and without pain. A friend of mine who voiced his dread of a lingering terminal illness said that he had prayed fervently for a quick end. His wife came home from a meeting one evening to find him sitting before the television set as though asleep. It was his final sleep.

Others linger long weeks or months or even years awaiting release. My grandfather said at the age of eighty that he was ready to go. At eighty-five he wondered how much longer he might have to wait. He suffered no serious illness, but was tired and wanted to regain the youth he was sure would be his when he entered that other dimension of time and space called heaven. At ninety he was growing a little impatient with God. "I wonder just what God is up to," he would say. At ninety-one he was still puzzled, but at ninety-three the end came as gently as a summer sunset.

Fear of the future can involve the ultimate fear of death, an inescapable fact of life which we are generally reluctant to discuss. In part the fear is a deep reluctance to leave the known for the unkown and a God-implanted instinct to cling to life. Two men were sharing their philosophies of life. One said, "I wonder what happens to us after death." The other replied, "Oh, I suppose we will go home to be with the Lord and dwell with him in eternal bliss, but why talk about such depressing things!"

This brings into sharp focus a common ambivalence about death and immortality. God has implanted within us a subtle but powerful longing for a continuation of this life and a pervasive belief in a continuation of life after death. Even the most primitive tribes believe in an "afterlife." There are, to use Wordsworth's term, "intimations of immortality" both within and without; yet, along with the hunger for heaven, there is in most of us an instinctive clinging to the known that is stronger than the yearning for another life. Most of us have dreamed wistfully of some far-off island-paradise where there are no alarm clocks, no freeways or smog, no schedules or irritations, where life is leisurely and unhurried. There is nothing wrong with such a dream. This could be the God-infused pull of another shore, which is heaven, or a part of the "collective unconscious," to employ Jung's term, a diffused racial memory of the Garden of Eden into which man was born as well as the home which is our destiny.

Two Who "Returned"

I once related in a sermon the experience of a woman I had known in Chicago. She had been in good health, except for a chronic heart condition which did not limit her normal activities. One evening I received word that she had been taken to the Billings Memorial Hospital for an emergency operation. I called on her after the operation. As I entered the room, she looked up and smiled, "Sit down. I want to talk to you. Something very unusual happened, and I want to share it with you." She took my hand and said, "Look, I'm not delirious or hallucinating. I was never more rational, and what I am about to tell you has nothing to do with dreams. This was entirely different."

"What happened?"

"Well, I was suddenly seized with some very severe pains, and my own physician couldn't be reached. I was brought here to Billings, and because it was an emergency, a staff doctor operated immediately. I had been told by my doctor that my heart wouldn't stand a general anesthetic, but I was too weak to tell the surgeon who was preparing for the operation. Soon my body felt very light, and I had a sense of peace I had never experienced before. I was walking across a vast expanse of incredibly beautiful lawn, surrounded by trees. Without being told, I knew where I was. It was heaven."

She must have sensed something in my manner, for she added, "I don't expect you to believe this, but it *wasn't* a dream. Dreams have a different feel to them, another kind of fabric. I saw people walking toward me, and they all had a look of infinite peace. I was beginning to feel that same peace. I sensed that they had come to welcome me. I became aware of my surroundings and was surprised that heaven was so much like earth, only far, far more beautiful. Then," she continued, "just as those joyous people approached me, I suddenly felt that I had to go back. I didn't know why. Then I opened my eyes. It was the saddest moment of my life when I looked up and saw the faces of the doctor and the nurses. I love my husband and my daughter, but I desperately wanted to go back where I had experienced such exquisite peace and joy even if only for a few brief moments."

"I Will Never Fear Death Again"

Later she was told that her heart had stopped beating while the anesthetic was being administered. She was given an injection of adrenaline, and her heart began to beat again. She said, "In the brief time while they were frantically preparing the injection, I got a glimpse of what heaven is really like. I will never fear death again as long as I live."

After the service in which I related the incident, a woman met me at the door. She had tears in her eyes, but she was smiling. "That happened to me," she said, "but I have never told anyone."

"What happened?"

"That same thing, only slightly different, and for a longer period of time."

"Will you come in sometime this week and tell me about it?"

"Of course! I've always wanted to share it with someone, but I was afraid they'd think I was out of my mind. I didn't even tell my husband."

She dropped in later in the week and told me her story: "I was drinking a cup of coffee at home late one afternoon. Suddenly I felt quite ill and terribly nauseated. The family physician was called, and I was rushed to the hospital. They told me later that a blood vessel had ruptured, and I had gone into shock."

She remembered being taken to the hospital and being wheeled into a room, but before the doctor or nurse could do anything further, she lapsed into unconsciousness. "I left my body lying there on the bed, and I was above it, suspended, weightless. There was no pain, now, and I felt pulled gently in a certain direction. I could move without effort, by thought alone. I moved, or was being moved gently, slowly upward. Suddenly I began to see beautiful lights, which grew brighter and brighter. People were all around me now, and I knew they had been waiting for me. They surrounded me, these friends whom I had known, and greeted me with joy. Everyone was incredibly, unbelievably happy. I knew them all, and of course they knew me. They put their arms about me, loving me, welcoming me, and then I felt myself moved on to another group of friends. They also radiated this indescribable love and joy. There are just no words with which to describe the peace and joy and happiness and release I felt. We communicated nonverbally. Words were not necessary.

More Beyond

"After what seemed a long time of enjoying this exquisite peace and joy, I noticed more lights on beyond, as though there was much more yet to be experienced. I sensed without being told that I was just at the portals of heaven. And Christ was there! I didn't see him, but I felt his presence. It was like feeling a love-peace-joy presence impossible to put into words. His presence seemed to fill the whole area as an experience, and it evoked a feeling of such intensity that—well, I can't describe it."

Her eyes filled with tears, but they were tears of joy, and I sensed that she felt a painful nostalgia. Perhaps she was feeling what Jesus felt when he wept at the tomb of Lazarus, just before he called, "Lazarus, come forth!" For Jesus felt it necessary to call Lazarus back from the Elysian fields of everlasting joy, to walk the dusty streets of Bethany again for a few years, as a demonstration that death does not say the final word.

"Suddenly," she went on, "there was a terrible,

crushing weight over my entire body. Then I realized that it was simply that I was back in my physical body, experiencing atmospheric pressure and the weight of my body. I was weeping silently, and the nurse kept wiping away the tears and assuring me that everything was going to be all right. I couldn't tell her what happened, and I let her go on thinking I was in pain or afraid but they were tears of mingled joy and sadness —joy over what I had been permitted to experience briefly, and sadness over leaving it behind. It was disappointment over coming back to life, or what we humans call life, but I had experienced life on another level and wanted more of it. I wanted it again, the indescribable joy and peace and happiness and fulfillment—and above all, to feel that presence which I knew was Christ."

Her physician told her later that she had no measurable blood pressure when she entered the hospital. He had not expected her to return to life. As long as she lives here in this earthly dimension, she will always feel a nostalgic pain, a longing for the other shore on which she stood ever so briefly. She lives a happy and contented life by any human standard, but she tells me that she will always experience a certain indefinable sadness over not being "there," where all is joy and peace and where Light unfolds and keeps on pulsating in the distance as though to indicate that through the limitless reaches of the eternal now one can go on loving and learning, walking toward the light which is God and where the presence of Christ is felt inwardly as an unending benediction.

It occurred to me later that the two women had several things in common: both were highly intelligent, and, perhaps most significant, they were very warm, loving individuals. As I write this, I recall the words of Jesus as he prayed: "I thank thee, Father, Lord of heaven and earth, for hiding these things from the learned and wise, and revealing them to the simple" (Matt. 11:25, NEB).

Chapter 6

FEAR OF FAILURE

It is our best that he wants, not the dregs of our exhaustion. I think he must prefer quality to quantity. . . .

GEORGE MACDONALD

In a counseling session a man related a dream in which he found himself perched on the steeply slanted roof of a house. "I was sitting there," he said, "trying to keep from falling off. It took all of my strength just to stay where I was."

I asked him what he made of his dream. He said, "Well, I suppose the house represents my life as it usually does in my dreams. Being on the roof could mean that I am on top of things but that I'm just barely hanging on."

"What about the enormous exertion required to keep you on top of things?" I asked.

"Yes, that's something I had overlooked. I suppose the amount of effort I expend avoiding failure may account for the fact that I am excessively tired most of the time. I go to bed tired and get up exhausted."

"Were you aware of your great fear of failure?"

"Only in part," he replied. "That dream helps me to be even more aware of my lifelong fear of blowing it, of failing, of looking bad in the eyes of others. I imagine it originated in my childhood. My father was loving but very demanding and quite critical. I went to extreme lengths to win his approval. I don't think I ever felt I got his affirmation. When I was about thirty, he told me for the first time how proud he was of me. I felt nothing except a vague sense of wanting to say, 'It's too late.' I had succeeded reasonably well in life, but his approval meant nothing to me then."

Psychiatrist Karen Horney writes of self-hate and self-contempt: "We do not hate ourselves because we are worthless but because we are driven to reach beyond ourselves. The hatred . . . results from the discrepancy between what I would be and what I am. There is not only a split, but a *cruel and murderous battle*."[1]

Where do we get this urge to reach beyond ourselves? What is the source of this need to be superior, to win glory, to reach the heights? It does not spring from a feeling of superiority but rather from a sense of weakness and inferiority. The drive to excel is fundamentally a fear of being weak, unimportant, unknown, and unappreciated. No one condemns a legitimate drive to succeed or a wholesome fear of failure. Within normal bounds these are both creative. It is only when we are driven far beyond our capabilities by some neurotic need that it becomes a sickness.

Doing the Right Thing for the Wrong Reason

There are those who have been so badly damaged in childhood that, far from desiring great achievement, they would settle for a modest degree of happiness. A young minister at a retreat I conducted shared what he had discovered in the several days we were together. "I never succeeded in winning my father's love or approval," he said, "so I think it was to win God's approval that I entered the ministry. God, the supreme father, would surely affirm me, even if my earthly father did not. Of course, at the time I chose the ministry, I was far from recognizing this as a part of my motive."

I said, "If God had to wait for perfectly pure motives, he would certainly be short-handed."

"Yes," he replied, "I am not deprecating my second-rate motives. I'm glad I entered the ministry. It has been fulfilling, but honesty compels me to face the real reason for my choice." He had found a large measure of satisfaction and contentment although he could still feel the pain of his father's rejection.

A young married woman shared her desperation in a series of intensive counseling sessions. She was an alcoholic, and when her anxiety level rose, she would take drugs if she couldn't get alcohol. Any drug would do, either uppers or downers. She admitted to taking pills from the medicine cabinets of friends or from their purses. She was not in any sense a thief by nature. It was simply that her anxiety became so intense that she would go to any lengths to get something to allay it. The source of her enormous anxiety appeared to stem from her relationship with her mother. She could recall nothing but rejection and indifference from her. There had been no approval, no validation of her feelings, no affection, and now she was a highly attractive young woman with no self-worth. She felt herself to be an utter failure. She had an intense fear of living the rest of her life with such a poor self-image.

Since she had never been able to do more than talk intellectually about her feelings toward her mother, I encouraged her to express her lifelong hostility in the safety of my office. It was not that I encouraged her to hate her mother; I simply urged her to be honest about her feelings and to express them as David did on occasion (see Ps. 109). I read to her one of them in which the psalmist called on God to punish his enemy, to cause his children to become orphans begging in the streets, with no one to give them food. It is a vehement, hate-filled psalm, hardly suitable for devotional reading, but it is honest. Eventually she learned to verbalize the hostility she had felt all of her life and to express the vehemence and anger that had been suppressed since childhood.

We cannot confess to God that which we will not admit to ourselves. In encouraging her to feel the full force of her lifelong hostility, I was simply leading her gently into honesty with God and with herself. Then I said, "When all of the anger is up and fully expressed, some day you can let yourself feel the compassion that is down there underneath your hostility—compassion for a woman who was damaged by *her* parents and thus rendered an incomplete mother to you."

I asked a friend of mine, a highly successful minister, how much of his zeal stemmed from love of God and man and how much from fear of failure. He laughed and, exaggerating a little perhaps, said, "About one-tenth is for love of God and man, and nine-tenths is the result of a hysterical fear of failure." His honesty was refreshing. His father had been a very loving but obscure and relatively unsuccessful person, and my friend, reared in comparative poverty, had no intention of being "unknown, unhonored, and unsung."

Perfectionism Is Basically Neurotic

Perfectionism is, in most instances, a neurotic manifestation of deep anxiety and a strong fear of failure. There are certain professions where perfectionistic traits are required. I want my airplane pilot, for instance, to be a rabid perfectionist! I hope my surgeon will be afflicted in the same way, and so with my accountant and architect. The men who design and build bridges should be wedded to the principle of ultimate perfection, at least in their daily work. But when this trait is carried into the home and other relationships it can be disastrous. We must not expect perfection of ourselves or of others. Generalized perfectionism is often the result of overcompensating for feelings of weakness or inadequacy or of perfectionistic parents who demand the ultimate in performance. Fearing the judgment of such parents, the child usually reacts by striving to please and tries to reach all of the goals set for him. In some instances the child rebels and refuses to try. He wins the battle by defeating the demanding parents at their own game.

Dick's father was a critical, demanding, rejecting person who, having failed in his own profession, projected his own self-contempt upon everyone around him. Dick's mother was a querulous, carping little woman whom he was never able to please. At thirty, when I first knew him, Dick was a nervous wreck. He still lived at home, hating every minute of it, but fearing to leave the safety of the nest. His fear of failure was essentially that he wanted to please his parents, but they had him in a double-bind. Nothing he did ever pleased them. His father downgraded him, cut him down with sarcasm, all the while urging him to achieve more and more. If he succeeded in any endeavor, it was never enough. He should have done it differently or better.

With the emotional support of a Yokefellow group, Dick finally made the break and established his own home. He had succeeded reasonably well in his profession and, now that he is away from the parental double-bind, is making progress in the discovery of his own identity.

One of the most pervasive fears is not simply the possibility that we shall fail as workers or as parents or as sons and daughters, but that we shall fail to win the approval, affection, and acceptance of our fellows. Henry was a very competent young man with a pleasant personality, but his self-effacing manner suggested some ancient hurt in childhood. In one group session he shared it. "When I was a kid," he said, "I had a very big, hooked nose. The kids called me Parrot. Youngsters can be very cruel. I felt their rejection strongly and drew into myself. As much as possible I avoided the other children at school. It was too painful to be around them and risk their ridicule. As soon as I could save enough money, I had my nose operated on, and now their jibes are only a painful memory."

Though Henry will always retain some of the emotional scars of those childhood experiences, he has become a creative, happy young man. His determination not to be defeated by the circumstances of life enabled him to achieve a high degree of happiness. He now has what he was denied in childhood: the affection, acceptance, and approval of his peer group. With these he, or anyone else, can live an effective and creative life. Without them life can be devastating and defeating.

The Right to Be Wrong

A popular song has in it the phrase, "Everyone has the right to be wrong once." One of our greatest fears is that of being wrong and having to admit it. The only ones who can admit it without loss of face are the individuals who have achieved a strong sense of their own identity and a genuine sense of their own worth. For them to admit making a mistake is no big thing, but many find it extremely difficult. They will argue interminably and go to ridiculous lengths to maintain the illusion that they could not possibly be wrong.

I once knew a man quite well who had a fantastic need to be right. In an argument he would summarize things by shouting, "Don't dispute my word! I know what I'm talking about." In reality he had little basis for his dogmatic views as he read little and was a high-school dropout. His family reported that he was never known to have said, "I was wrong," or to admit having made a mistake. It simply never occurred to him that by the wildest stretch of the imagination he could be wrong. He could not afford to be wrong, for his self-worth was so small that it would have been devastating to have to confess to being less than omniscient.

A legitimate fear of failure can be a creative emotion. No one wants to do a sloppy job or have his achievement viewed with scorn by others. Our own sense of values should be enough to prevent us from

90

doing a second-rate job when we are capable of much more. It is only when the desire for excellence becomes obsessive that we err, or when we outreach ourselves, striving for goals beyond our abilities. I observed a young woman with modest musical abilities ruin her marriage, alienate her daughter, and destroy her health trying to achieve impossible goals. She ended life as a paranoid invalid, having taken to her bed in an effort to show the world that only her illness prevented her from succeeding.

Sibling Rivalry

Sometimes the fear of failure is based on sibling rivalry. As a young girl, Sybil became aware that, as she put it, "Boys were better." She felt that her older brother was given preferential treatment. His grades were better, and thus he was the one who was sent to college. She stayed at home to help with the rearing of several younger children. A passive person might have accepted this with quiet resignation, but Sybil was anything but passive. As soon as she could, she fled from home, secured a job in a nearby city, and proceeded to try to make her mark in the world. Without being aware of it at the time, she was competing with her brother for her parents' approval. He had been given their approval without effort. Sybil broke all records for achievement in the next few years, unwittingly seeking the affirmation denied her in childhood. In a relatively short time she became a department store buyer, then was promoted to the position of assistant manager. She had spent virtually all of her psychic energy in her all-out effort to achieve success. There had been little time left for friends or social activities.

When I first knew her, she was a tense, rather brittle, lonely woman of thirty-four. She had achieved a measure of success but was bitter and unfulfilled. I asked if her parents had ever given her the approval she sought. "No," she said, "all I get from them is appeals for money. They're hard up. My brother has a family;

so they don't ask him for financial help. They expect me to go on taking care of them indefinitely. I still haven't won their love—only the right to send them a check every month. And on top of that, they still want to run my life. They still give me advice and check on my social activities."

Sybil was still trying to win love and approval from parents who had none to give. I encouraged her to give up the competition with her brother and find satisfaction in other directions. "Even if you were to outstrip your brother in achievements," I said, "what would you gain?"

"Some personal satisfaction, at least."

"Would revenge be a better word?"

She looked startled. "I don't think I'm out for revenge—well, maybe I am. At least I've been determined to show him and my parents that I'm every bit as good as he is."

"Having proven it, as you now have, what has it gained you?"

"Nothing, except the inner satisfaction of knowing that I'm not a second-rater."

"Can you accept that and set some other goals now?"

"Like what?"

"What about friends?"

"I have no close friends."

"Would you like some?"

"I've been too busy succeeding to spend my time on close friendships, but," she looked wistful, "I do feel very lonely when I get home at night. My apartment is every bit as nice as my brother's, but that doesn't give me as much satisfaction as I thought it would."

Eventually, Sybil abandoned her futile struggle to out-do her brother and set some new goals for herself. There had been no time for men in her life, partly because her hostility toward her brother had become a generalized hatred of all men. Feeding the flames of her hostility toward males was the awareness that she had never won her father. Some fairly extensive counseling eventually enabled her to see the futility of permitting her hostility toward her father and brother to mar her life. She found herself being less and less interested in Women's Lib activities and more and more attracted to men. In time she married and, after working on some vestigial remains of hostility toward all males, worked out a good marital relationship.

Expressing Love to Parents

A friend of mine was speaking to a crowd of about eighty high-school students about love. He asked them how long it had been since they had said, "I love you," to their parents. There was silence. He then challenged them to express love directly and verbally, to say, "I love you" to their parents. Only one of the eighty seemed willing. The others agreed with one young man who said rather hesitantly, "I'm not sure how they'd take it." These young people all needed love, and of course their parents needed it just as badly. Despite our knowledge that love is the medicine for the healing of the world, many of us often find it very difficult to utter those three magic words, "I love you."

Lack of love creates great anxiety in infant, child, and adult. Dr. H. V. Scott of Ft. Wayne, Indiana, told me of an incident concerning a mother and her one-year-old baby. The mother had become somewhat depressed although no one around her was aware of it. The only evidence of her depression was a certain detachment. She did all of the necessary things for the baby—fed and diapered him and saw that he was taken care of in a general way—but she didn't hold him as much as formerly. The baby began to lose weight and ceased to smile. He became depressed in response to the mother's depression. The baby also exhibited other signs of anxiety. Dr. Scott put the baby in the hospital and told the nurses to touch and hold and cuddle him as much as possible. Almost immediately the baby began to gain weight and in a short time gave every evidence of being normal. Meanwhile the mother's heretofore undetectable depression was delt with, and as soon as she was her normal self again, the baby was given back to her.

Dr. Scott said that he had occasion to follow the child's course for a number of years. The infant grew into a high-school student who is bright and normal in every way. The doctor's feeling was that the baby had simply felt the mother's depression, even before anyone else noticed it, and reacted accordingly, becoming depressed and anxious in response to the mother's feelings.

Misunderstanding Gifts

Love is sometimes misinterpreted. A man told me that for a long time when he gave his wife gifts she seemed quite unresponsive. She would give little or no response except to say, "Oh, that's nice." He never knew why she seemed so indifferent. In a Yokefellow group she shared in one session the fact that her mother was unable to express love but substituted gifts. As a girl she wanted her mother's love, not gifts. Suddenly both she and her husband began to see why his gifts had always been received with comparative indifference. Gifts to her were a substitute for love and had no meaning.

I asked him, "Now that she understands the source of her reaction, does she enjoy receiving gifts from you?"

"Yes," he said, "her response is quite different. Now she knows that the gifts are an expression of love, not a substitute. She is most responsive."

We have over six hundred thousand words in the English language and more synonyms per word than are found in any other language. However, we have only one word with which to express all of the various shadings of love. Although there are sixteen major categories of love, we are still dependent upon one word with which to convey all of those various meanings. Deficient as is our language in this respect, it is

94

still possible to convey a world of meaning, by inflection and otherwise, in the words, "I love you."

Emmet Fox once said:

There is no difficulty that enough love will not conquer; no disease that enough love will not heal; no door that enough love will not open; no gulf that enough love will not bridge; no wall that enough love will not throw down; no sin that enough love will not redeem.

It makes no difference how deeply seated may be the trouble, how hopeless the outlook, how muddled the tangle, how great the mistake, a sufficient realization of love will dissolve it all. If only you could love enough you would be the happiest and most powerful being in the world.[2]

Six Fundamental Needs

There are any number of lists of inner needs or hierarchies of values. Each of us might, out of our own experience, make up our own. On the basis of some forty-odd years of counseling and observation, I have come to believe that the following six needs are fundamental:

Survival (the need to have continued existence)
Security (economic and emotional)
Sex (as an expression of love; as a sexual being)
Significance (to amount to something; to be worth-while)
Self-fulfillment (to achieve fulfilling goals)
Selfhood (a sense of identity)

Failure to find expression of these needs can produce anything from frustration to devastation.

Survival. The fundamental need for survival is obvious. The human organism has any number of built-in mechanisms to assure probable survival. These mechanisms range from the capacity of the body to maintain an even temperature despite climatic changes, to the self-healing process whereby a wound tends to cleanse and heal itself by an amazingly complex series of activities on the part of the entire organism. A hundred thousand activities are involved in the process whereby the physical body, not to mention the emotional structure, maintains stasis—a kind of balance of all the variable forces involved in the life process.

Security. For many thousands of years man maintained a fairly precarious existence. His chief goal was to survive, which meant to acquire the creature necessities (comforts came later if at all) of food and shelter. As life became less a daily struggle for bare existence, there arose the need for emotional security. One can feel emotionally safe only if relationships and the environment are relatively stable and satisfying. The future needs to seem comparatively nonthreatening if one is to have emotional security. It is interesting that the fundamental need of a typical woman is for security. This involves not only economic factors but the stability provided by a close family unit. Ideally this includes husband, children, home, and enough money to maintain the operation. A man's basic need is for affection in the form of sex, approval, and acceptance. Surprisingly, economic security tends to fall into second place for a typical male.

Sex. Taken in the broader context, sex involves one's identity as a sexual being, the fulfilling of the sexual role as defined by nature and one's culture. In the narrower sense it involves sexual expression in the love-sex act. It is probable that Freud was not far wrong when he named sex as the strongest of the drives. Certainly it is one of the most fundamental of all our instinctual urges. Physically and emotionally it seems to loom large as a basic need. But in my opinion Freud missed the mark when he failed to take into consideration the spiritual side of man. If we involve the spiritual aspect of man's nature, there is another urge more basic than the sex drive which is all-embracing—selfhood.

Significance. Alfred Adler broke with Freud over, among other things, the primacy of the sex drive. Adler felt that the fundamental drive was not sex but the need to compensate for our feelings of inferiority, to achieve significance. This is most certainly a basic need. It is perceived in very young children, in youth, in the middleaged, and in the elderly. We seem almost never to lose the need to be significant, to be noticed, to win approval in some form. Most of our drive to succeed in any given realm is based on our need for approval and a concomitant need to avoid disapproval. It begins early in life and ends only when, in later years, the man retires with a pension, a gold watch, or a scroll attesting to his "worth" to the company; or in the case of a typical woman, with the assurance that she has succeeded as a mother and can relax in the love and adoration of her grandchildren. They have "achieved something worthwhile." The innate fear of failure and a longing for the rewards of success as defined by our culture have provided sufficient motivation to keep them moving in the direction of achievement, recognition, and/or power.

Self-fulfillment. This is somewhat different from significance although at times the lines of demarcation may blur. Achieving some measure of significance can provide one with a degree of satisfaction and self-fulfillment. But the all-embracing aspect of fulfillment includes those areas defined as happiness, contentment (that close relative of happiness for which most of us are quite willing ultimately to settle), and a deep sense of satisfaction. For some this may include such things as job satisfaction, a satisfying marital relationship, producing and rearing children who "turn out well," hobbies, gratifying social relationships, and the realization of certain goals. Those whose goals were out of harmony with their talents or opportunities are often frustrated and unhappy even though they may have attained goals which would satisfy others. It is not so much the size of the achievement that gives one satisfaction as whether it is fairly close to earlier childhood dreams and aspirations.

Thus, a youngster who loves animals and butterflies and dreams of being a biologist or zoologist may be perfectly content if he can end up teaching biology at the high-school level. Someone else whose dreams of glory were far more grandiose may despise such attainments and be frustrated and unhappy if he cannot write the world's greatest treatise on the life cycle of the tsetse fly and become a full professor at one of the larger universities.

Selfhood. This has to do with the ultimate questions: Who am I? Why am I here? How can I discover my true identity? And discovering it, how can that identity be fulfilled to the utmost? This seems to me to be more fundamental and basic than the sex drive, as postulated by Freud, or the need for significance, as suggested by Adler, or the "will to meaning" which Frankl believed to be the basic human drive. I see selfhood as being more basic because it involves the physical, mental, and spiritual aspects of an individual and because it embraces Freud's, Adler's, and Frankl's drives, then goes somewhat beyond. Since selfhood involves the spiritual side of man as well as the physical and mental, the search for one's true identity involves even the final questions: Is there survival after death? Is man a spirit possessing a body and a mind, or is he simply a physical organism seeking sexual gratification, or significance, or the meaning of life?

More Than Sex, Fulfillment, and Meaning

I prefer to believe that man is a spirit, created of the same essence as God and possessed of some of the attributes of God, though on a diminished scale; that man is encapsulated in a human body which one day disintegrates and returns to dust; that he inhabits this little planet for a short time before moving on to another dimension of time and space; that in other realms beyond our imagination he will carry on his search for growth and fulfillment; that in the end he will discover his ultimate identity—his selfhood—as he becomes perfected through the aeons and finally senses through some inner light that he is ready for the final steps—to affirm his complete oneness with God as Jesus did.

How well we function in achieving any of these goals or needs seems to depend in large measure upon how well we like ourselves. We have a right to love ourselves properly. Jesus said that one aspect of the supreme law was, "You shall love your neighbor as *yourself.*" The clear implication is that a proper self-love is expected, for if we do not love ourselves, we will project onto others our own self-hate in the form of criticism and hostility.

A child reared in a perfect home environment (I do not know of any) would receive love and affirmation but would be taught to *give* love too, for without learning how to love, a child is severely limited. Such a child would have a strong self-image. He would respect and love himself properly. His identity would have been validated. He would have self-worth. Since all of us lacked a perfect home environment, to some degree we grew up lacking identity. Feelings of inferiority resulted. In an effort to compensate for these feelings of inferiority, tensions were created in the personality. So one *must* find a way to compensate, to achieve a sense of being worthwhile.

A typical individual, in order to achieve this sense of being worthwhile, will set some goal. Achieving this goal will supposedly give him immense satisfaction. He will feel "satisfied"—"I do amount to something after all." Unfortunately, having achieved that goal, he usually perceives that there is something lacking. He has confused his role as a husband and wage earner with his true identity. A woman may confuse her role as wife and mother with her true identity. When such a man retires and the woman's children have left home, neither has any genuine identity or true sense of being worthwhile. Their only worth lay in the fact that the man spent forty years working for Amalgamated Tool and Die Company and the woman can point to four children and eleven grandchildren, all of whom are doing well. *Their attainments are all outside themselves.*

We need not deprecate such achievements though they are not the ultimate. They correspond to the four-by-fours which might be used to support a house while a permanent concrete foundation is being poured. The four-by-fours will support the house for the time being and in fact are necessary, but they are not intended to be permanent supports for the house. In the same way, job success or success in rearing a family—good and necessary as they are—were never intended to provide a genuine sense of identity. One's identity must be *within oneself*. It has little to do with external achievements. These are by-products.

Acquiring a Sense of Identity

How then does one go about acquiring a true sense of identity, a sense of selfhood? Perhaps no two persons ever arrived there by identical routes, but in general these factors seem to be essential:

First, one must become acutely aware that we are more than physical beings; that we are, indeed, akin to the angels, made in the image of God; that we are immortal; that this life is but a single chapter in what may be a very large book. As a spiritual being one recognizes the importance of the physical, for God created our physical world and loves his handiwork. But at best it is temporal, as are our material bodies. When our bodies return to dust, there remains a spiritual self which is indestructible since it is created in the image of God.

Second, one must seek for integrity. The Bible calls it wholeness. Jesus did not ask people if they wanted him to make them holy, but he did ask frequently, "Do you want to be made *whole?*" Our term for this would be *integrated*—to have our minds, spirits, and bodies working harmoniously, without conflict. Achieving this requires integrity. Integrity involves such things as utter honesty, complete humility, and genuine love for God and man. It is comforting to know that God does not expect absolute perfection or total humility or complete honesty. If he did, few if any of us would make it. But the goal is there. To the degree that we can attain that goal we find our selfhood; and to that degree the aching, lonely, dissatisfied, unfulfilled self can find contentment and peace.

Though rejected and despised, Jesus expressed the hope "that my joy may be in you, and that your joy may be full" (John 15:11, RSV). His sense of inner joy and peace sprang, not from outward circumstances, but from an inner peace. He was whole. He wholly accepted his divinity and completely accepted his humanity. Since he integrated these and became fully man and fully God, even crucifixion could not rob him of the knowledge that "I and the Father are one" (John 10:30, RSV).

Chapter 7

THE ANXIOUS PERSONALITY

Not in the clamor of the crowded street,
Not in the shouts and plaudits of the throng,
But in ourselves, are triumph and defeat.

LONGFELLOW

At a seminar where I was speaking, someone in the audience asked what my next book was going to be about. I said, "It will deal with release from fear and anxiety." From the back of the room came a woman's anguished voice, "Hurry!" There was laughter, but everyone knew that excessive anxiety is no laughing matter.

Anxiety can be defined as a generalized state of apprehension, accompanied by restlessness and tension, for which there is no apparent cause. The anxious personality is one which, for a variety of reasons, is afflicted with this generalized tension and apprehension. Such a person lacks inner peace and serenity. In the child the symptoms may include nail biting, bed wetting, stuttering, shortened attention span, restlessness, aberrant behavior, temper tantrums, and difficulty in concentrating. Such a child is often termed hyperkinetic (overactive). The label is a description of the symptomatic behavior, not a diagnosis of the problem.

The adult with an anxiety neurosis may be a compulsive worker, eater, drinker, talker, or gambler; he may be restless and dissatisfied, with sundry emotional and/or physical complaints. He may in some instances go from job to job or marriage to marriage searching for "the ultimate" which seems to elude him. The list of symptoms is legion. We legitimately experience anxiety momentarily when something poses a threat to our security, peace of mind, self-image, pride, our general well-being, or the realization of some goal. But the clue lies in the word *momentarily*. When the threat disappears, the anxiety level should subside.

In some instances anxiety can prove a creative force in one's life. For instance, Leonardo da Vinci, who possessed one of the most versatile minds of all time, was illegitimate. This was considered to be a terrible stigma by his contemporaries. According to some of his biographers, his lowly birth undoubtedly was a factor which spurred him toward greater achievement. Very often an inferiority complex generates sufficient anxiety to provide a stimulus to significant achievement.

Anxiety is experienced not only in humans but apparently in lower forms of life as well. Suzanne K. Langer, in *Mind—An Essay on Human Feelings,* writes of "reactive behavior in the rising and sinking of plankton in adjustment to light conditions, to day and night surface temperature of the water. . . . Vertical migration provides the animal, otherwise drifting at the mercy of the environment, with the mechanism for changing that environment for another."[1] This infinitesimally small sea creature reacts to anxiety "produced by water that is too hot or too cold, too bright or too dark, acid or alkaline, as a power of choice." It might be argued that the reaction of plankton to light and dark, heat and cold, is not in response to anxiety but is simply "reactive behavior," but that is, of course, one of the aspects of what we humans term *anxiety*.

Nine hundred years ago an Arab scholar, Ali Ibn Hazm, stated that no one ever makes any decision or choice or does anything at all except as the result of anxiety. In other words, every human action or reaction is in response to the survival factor called anxiety. It is only when anxiety becomes excessive or all-pervasive that it becomes a negative rather than a positive force.

Anxiety as experienced by humans is at least 2.8 million years old, according to very recent anthropological discoveries. The discovery in Kenya of humanoid bones and a skull, carbon dated at 2.8 million years, pushes the antiquity of man back by millennia. Modern man, who until recently was not supposed to have existed until around 35,000 B.C., now appears to have developed as early as one hundred thousand years ago, and his progenitors, nearly three million years before.

Primitive Man Had Anxiety

If dodging traffic, fighting smog, and enduring the tensions caused by a proliferation of choices have been a source of anxiety for modern man, consider the situation of man one hundred thousand years ago. He had no permanent home, not yet having developed farming. His survival depended upon finding animals for food. In one sense life was very simple, but in other ways, quite complicated. The entire tribe or family had to move when the supply of game animals was exhausted. Man had few if any defenses against the elements. His life span, up to and including the Middle Ages, was quite brief. He had no defense against disease, no treatment for accidents. Daily life was a constant struggle for survival. Anxiety is nothing new. It is as old as life on earth. It is a benevolent provision of God, a survival factor, a danger-alert system aimed at protecting life. In normal amounts it is of God. In excessive amounts it can be disastrous.

In *Man's Search for Himself*, Rollo May says that modern anxiety is partially due to man's inability to express his deepest emotions. He suggests that emotional spontaneity and honesty open man's hidden strengths, but man buries his true self in an image of what he would like to be. Love and hate, he says, are the two emotions most often denied.[2]

Achieving Self-worth

One major source of excessive anxiety is the failure to achieve a sense of self-worth or identity. Dr. William Glasser, in *Schools without Failure*,[3] says that, "Love and self-worth are so intertwined that they may properly be related through the use of the term identity. The single basis that people have is the requirement for an identity; the belief that we are someone in distinction to others, and that the someone is important and worthwhile. Then love and self-worth may be considered the two pathways that man has discovered lead to a successful identity." There are not many kinds of failure, Glasser believes. There are only two: the failure to give and receive love, and the failure to achieve self-worth; but these two are so closely related, he says, that it is difficult to separate them.

If a child has failed to learn to love, as an adult he finds it very difficult, though not impossible, to love. An adult who is capable of giving and receiving love has a much better chance of succeeding in almost any endeavor. The child who was spoiled and pampered and given an excessive amount of unconditional love is in as difficult a position as the child who received no love at all; for the pampered child will go through life wondering why the world fails to give him the unconditional love he received from his parents.

The anxious personality is more likely to suffer from heart disease, peptic ulcer, irritability, excessive tension and restlessness, lack of appetite or excessive appetite, migraine headaches, asthma, and a score of other physical and emotional symptoms. But telling the anxiety-prone individual not to worry, to relax, is roughly as effective as telling someone with a broken leg to stop limping. In fact, it is much easier to recover from a broken leg than from an anxiety neurosis. Since the anxiety is invisible, it is difficult for observers to be understanding. They are in the same position as depressed persons whom an unsympathetic world tells to "snap out of it. Look on the bright side of things."

It is probable that the person with an anxiety neurosis is born with a central nervous system which makes it much easier for him to form conditioned responses. That is, his autonomic nervous system is overreactive. Such a tendency makes him more prone than others to develop responses which we term neurotic symptoms. Thus the anxiety-ridden individual is not to condemn himself for his tension and other symptoms, nor should friends and relatives expect him to alter his basic reactions as the result of admonitions to "slow down, take it easy, don't be so tense and nervous."

That there is a possible correlation between anxiety and cancer is the opinion of Dr. Claus Bahnson, a psychologist, and Dr. George F. Solomon, a Stanford University psychiatrist. There is an important emotional component in cancer, these two men assert. Fear of one's emotions, they believe, can play a significant part in one's susceptibility to cancer. The cancer-prone personality, Bahnson says, is not able to handle stress well. He has trouble expressing anger and other emotions and does not have channels for emotional discharge. Thus the anxiety-ridden personality who is bottled up emotionally is somewhat more likely to be a cancer victim. Excessive anxiety, however, is productive of more than one disease. It can lay the groundwork for any number of physical symptoms.

The Age of Anxiety

The person with an anxiety neurosis can point with some justification to certain well-documented facts which make ours an age of anxiety. As pointed out by Alvin Toffler,[4] a little over a hundred years ago there were only 19 cities with a population of one million. By 1960 there were 141 such cities. One-half of all the energy consumed by man in the last two thousand years has been consumed in the last one hundred years.

Five thousand years ago the maximum speed that could be attained was by a camel caravan traveling eight miles per hour. By 1500 B.C. the chariot developed a speed of twenty miles an hour. In 1880 the steam locomotives had a speed of one hundred miles per hour. By 1938 planes could travel four hundred miles per hour, and by 1960 there were planes which attained a speed of four thousand miles per hour. In the late sixties space capsules reached a speed of eighteen thousand miles per hour. Not only has the world speeded up in terms of travel, but in a hundred other ways. Before A.D. 1500, as Toffler points out, in all of Europe books were produced at the rate of one thousand titles per year. By 1950, one hundred twenty thousand titles annually were being produced. By 1970, three hundred sixty-five thousand titles per year were being produced. The U.S. government alone turns out one hundred thousand reports and four hundred fifty thousand books, articles, and papers annually.

The world is moving very fast in science, social change, education, government, transportation—in fact in almost every area of knowledge and human activity. The end result is, for many people, a kind of free-floating anxiety. What will come next? What about the hydrogen bomb? Or inflation? The future? In a sense it can be said that the individual who lacks some anxiety in today's world just doesn't know what is happening.

On my way to the ancient "lost city of Petra" I stopped for the night at a hotel in Amman, Jordan. As I signed the guest register, I glanced at the clock on the wall, then at my wrist watch. "Did you know your clock is five minutes slow?" I asked the desk clerk. He said, with calm indifference, "What's five minutes in the Hashemite Kingdom of the Jordan?" On my return from Petra I spent the night at the same hotel. I glanced at the wall clock again. It was now twenty minutes late.

The desk clerk saw my glance, and we smiled together. I said, "What's twenty minutes in the Hashemite Kingdom of the Jordan?"

Promptness can be either a virtue or a neurosis. Both the compulsively "on time" personality and the perpetually late individual suffer from anxiety. Their anxiety just takes different forms. The anxious personality more often than not has a pathological fear of being late. He may be the first to arrive. He may also be a picture straightener, a lint picker, a fidgeter, and usually has some mild to severe compulsion which is not so evident. Though he may make life miserable or at least uncomfortable for others, he really makes it harder for himself but does not know how to stop his anxious, compulsive behavior pattern. In the last chapter we deal with some of the better-known means for achieving some release of these symptoms; but for the moment it is best simply to describe and identify the anxious personality.

The Leisureliness of Jesus

What was the secret of the leisureliness of Jesus, who had only three short years in which to work, yet managed to carry on his mission without stress or anxiety? He arrived four days or more late for the funeral of Lazarus, an intimate friend, and offered no explanation for his delay. A sister of Lazarus, upon his arrival, said, "Lord, if you had been here, my brother would not have died" (John 11:21, RSV), but there was no defensiveness in his reply. He was sufficiently free of anxiety to stop in the midst of his discourse to a large crowd and invite noisy little children to come and talk to him.

Mark records what must have been a rather confused scene: Jesus and the twelve had just returned by boat from across the lake, and "a great crowd gathered about him." Apparently he was about to address them, or minister to them in some way; but Jairus, a ruler of the synagogue, "fell at his feet, and besought him, saying, 'My little daughter is at the point of death. Come and lay your hands on her, so that she may be made well, and live.' And he went with him." A great throng followed him, and on the way to the home of Jairus a woman desiring healing touched the hem of his garment and was healed. Jesus "perceiving in himself that power had gone forth from him, turned about in the crowd, and said, 'Who touched my garments?' " The woman came in fear and trembling confessed that she had been the one. He said, "Daughter, your faith has made you well; go in peace, and be healed of your disease." (Mark 5:21-34, RSV).

First there was the crowd that gathered at the water's edge; then came Jairus with his urgent plea; then the woman's interruption. In the midst of a crowd, among whom must have been many seeking his attention, beset by interruptions and noise and the confusion that is always present in a mob of people, Jesus remained calm and unhurried. St. Vincent de Paul said, "Haste delays the things of God." Jesus seems never to have been hurried or harried.

Could the secret of his inner peace be that he was at peace with himself, that there was no inner disharmony to mar the placidity of his spirit, no ambivalence and thus no tension? He knew who he was, and in accepting fully his humanity, and his divinity, there was no loss of psychic energy such as is usually experienced with inner conflict or uncertainty. Could a part of his secret be that he alternated between periods of intense activity and times of receptivity when he went out alone "a great while before dawn" to pray? How passionately we protest that we have no time for meditation and prayer; how fervently we plead busyness as an excuse to avoid the daily quiet time. A man who belongs to five committees, three boards, and two clubs will declare that he simply has no time in his life for meditation; and he is quite right. He doesn't have the time, for he has filled every chink of time with "busy work" in a frantic and unconscious effort to allay the anxiety that gnaws at him.

A woman with three jobs at church, four children, a bridge club, and a Cub Scout den will proclaim to the world that she is too busy, as indeed she is. By going where she is pushed, she avoids God and her inner self. The individual who is too selfish to become involved at all with others, and is bored, will say that he just hasn't the temperament for meditation, or that he tried it and it didn't do any good, or that he had too much religion when he was young. The truth is far different: we are afraid of God. We don't like him and avoid him, and we fear to look within even for ten minutes a day, for it might involve some reorganization of our lives, or the straightening out of relationships, or the admission that our values are all wrong. We go to any lengths to avoid that, and we search hopefully for just the right panacea to allay the anxiety that is there day and night.

Being Rushed and Overbusy

Elizabeth Prentiss once said, "If you could once make up your mind in the fear of God never to take on more work of any sort than you can carry on calmly, quietly, without hurry or flurry, and the instant you feel yourself growing nervous, and like one out of breath, would stop and take breath, you would find this simple common-sense rule doing for you what no prayers or tears could ever accomplish."[5] I am well aware of that principle, but some ancient tape is still running in my head urging me to say yes to everyone, to take on every job offered, to refuse no request. That is a parent tape, and it will keep on playing as long as I live. With the years the sound of it has become muted. Here and there I have succeeded in rerecording the tape. One can be grateful even for occasional victories.

Normally I feel a great urge to be on time for everything. I formerly rationalized it as an act of courtesy and as being responsible. This is true, but the real reason I was compulsively on time, or early, is that I was

111

programed that way. I came to realize that I had been early for monthly denominational board meetings an entire year but that the meetings always started eighteen to twenty minutes after the announced time. I decided to break a lifetime habit. I began to arrive fifteen minutes late, and invariably the board members were just beginning to assemble in a relaxed and leisurely fashion. I estimate that at those and other meetings in twenty years I saved hundreds of hours. It wasn't easy. I was running counter to a very loud tape and against a neurotic sense of responsibility. Flushed with success over that one victory, I proceeded to apply it to other areas of my life. It worked wherever I was able to apply it. It is probable that the anxious personality can scarcely hope to be rid of all his neurotic behavior patterns at once. On the contrary he may congratulate himself if he can win one victory, major or minor, every few months or even once a year. There is no need to give up hope or become discouraged if the anxiety patterns hang on desperately. They die hard, as do all old habits. Be as patient with yourself as you would with another person. This can be a great virtue. For if you can be kind and loving and forgiving to yourself, you will then find it much, much easier to relate to others in the same spirit.

Much anxiety is generated in the anxious personality by a need to be "guarded." The guarded personality is, consciously or unconsciously, afraid that his secret will be discovered. He spends a vast amount of psychic energy guarding his secret. It may be that he is an angry person and has spent a lifetime pretending to be saccharine sweet, in which case he is usually unaware of the pretense. Or it may be a generalized and largely unconscious fear that other emotions will get out of control. Thus he invests a great deal of energy in maintaining a false front, the pretense that he is not like that at all. On the contrary, he assures himself and everyone else that he is the calm, unemotional, unperturbed person his parents required him to be.

112

Some of our guilty secrets involve real guilt, but often there is no guilt at all. I recall a timid young woman in an all-day seminar. During an exchange in which some emotions were expressed she left the room in tears. Half an hour later when she had not returned, I went to look for her. I found her weeping unconsolably. Finally I was able to get from her the fact that something had triggered an old guilt, one so great that she had never shared it with her husband. She insisted she couldn't divulge the terrible secret. Eventually, however, I induced her to share it, assuring her that she could get great relief by dredging up the painful memory. It turned out that the "guilt" had to do with the fact that her brother and father fought constantly, and she was never able to stop them. She felt enormously guilty about this. She had always hated violence and felt guilty over not getting her brother and father to love each other. I took the better part of an hour to get her to see, at least intellectually, that there was no guilt involved. Consider how much of an investment she had made in terms of psychic energy in keeping that "secret guilt" to herself.

One manifestation of excessive anxiety is observed in the compulsive individual. Whether it is expressed in overeating, overdrinking, overworking, overachieving, or whatever, such forms of excessiveness can nearly always be traced back to the fact that the child was not loved enough, or at least not in an acceptable form. The inner child of the past, always present in the adult, still does not feel loved. The deprivation was in the past, but the hurt is in the person in the present. Time in no way diminishes the need for love. Thus, excessive anxiety at its source is the unfulfilled need of the infant for limitless, unconditional love. Though it may not rise to consciousness so that one can say, "I feel vaguely unfulfilled because of a deprivation of love in childhood," it is expressed unconsciously in such forms as compulsive buying, eating, drinking, collecting, achieving, working, aggressive driving, aberrant sexual behavior, ad infinitum. These and many other compulsive behavior patterns are an effort to relieve the anxiety which has been there since childhood.

We are not to blame our parents, but we can get the guilt off our own backs and trace it to the source. Our parents can trace their human inadequacies back to *their* parents, and so on back to the Garden of Eden. There is no one to blame, least of all ourselves. We are to blame ourselves only if we are unwilling to take the necessary steps to resolve our difficulties. We are not responsible for the past; we *are* responsible for the future and what we do with it.

Chapter 8

ANXIETY—NORMAL AND NEUROTIC

*Oh, to grasp this sorry scheme of things
entire, shatter it to bits, and remold it near
to the heart's desire.*

OMAR KHAYYAM

Craig is a good illustration of generalized anxiety which
can become destructive. He was about seventeen when
his parents induced him to come in for counseling. He
was a nice looking, languid, excessively passive young
man. The family had considerable wealth, and the
youngster had associated almost entirely with boys
from wealthy homes. In the private school which he
attended the use of drugs was almost universal. Craig
told me with no reluctance whatever that he had used
uppers, downers, pot, "hard stuff" (heroin), and alcohol. He had been hospitalized for a serious ailment
resulting from drug abuse, and his physician had told
him that continued use of drugs would almost certainly
prove fatal.

Craig had neither motivation, ambition, nor goals.
Beneath his seemingly calm exterior and gentle pas-
sivity there must lurk, I felt, a seething cauldron of
anxiety. The human organism is normally so constituted
as to prompt an individual to find some creative outlet
for his physical and mental energies. The very culture
in which we live is anxiety-producing in that it stresses

the acquisition of material things; but Craig's normal needs were being met without effort on his part, and he was frustrated because there appeared to be no goal worth working for. Since he was deeply frustrated, he was terribly anxious, but the anxiety did not reveal itself in his calm personality. It showed only in his compulsive need for anxiety-allaying drugs.

At one point Craig said, reflecting upon his life situation, "Sometimes I wish I had grown up in a less-privileged home, so I could have some goals to work toward. As it is, all of my needs are met. What do I have to look forward to, to work for?"

The drug culture of today, with its tens of thousands of ruined lives, is to be deplored. But what about the basic cause of the anxiety which creates the need for a drug to alleviate the tension? Granted that the causes are complex, it still behooves us to glance at the source rather than to deal with the symptoms. Among the myriad causes of emotional stress and anxiety among people today, these certainly deserve mention: the Vietnam War of the late '60s and early '70s; the decreasing emphasis upon moral and spiritual values, which manifests itself in crime, and its depiction in TV and movies; the threat of an all-out atomic war; the sexual revolution with its "anything goes" approach; and of course, the overemphasis upon purely material values. Many young people have rebelled against our materialistic society. In a sense, some of them have backed away from the ditch and fallen over the cliff; they have overreacted. We still live in a material world, and if a foolish overemphasis upon material values has developed, the answer does not appear to be found in a vacant-eyed, slack-jawed, drug-induced euphoria, a state of stoned nonbeing.

Our Anxiety-producing Culture

Alvin Toffler, in *Future Shock,* points out that, "We are simultaneously experiencing a youth revolution, a sexual revolution, a racial revolution, a colonial revolution, an economic revolution, and the most rapid and deep-going technological revolution in history."[1] According to the chief White House adviser on urban affairs, the United States "exhibits the qualities of an individual going through a nervous breakdown."

As if these things were not enough to provide excessive overstimulation, the knowledge explosion is almost unbelievable. Dr. Robert Hilliard, the top educational broadcasting specialist for the Federal Communications Commission, says, "At the rate at which knowledge is growing, by the time the child born today graduates from college, the amount of knowledge in the world will be four times as great. By the time that child is fifty years old, it will be thirty-two times as great, and 97 percent of everything known in the world will have been learned since the time he was born."[2] There is a vast difference between knowledge and wisdom. A great deal of wisdom will be required to discover ways in which this enormous proliferation of facts can be used constructively.

Indicative of the increased tension and anxiety affecting society is the fact that "at British universities roughly twenty percent of the undergraduates seek psychiatric assistance at some time during their three-year course of study. For some, the situation becomes unbearable and suicides are unusually frequent, the university rate being three to six times higher than the national average for the same group. At Oxford and Cambridge universities, the suicide rate is seven to ten times higher."[3]

Anxiety, Shame and Guilt

Another source of excessive anxiety is guilt, in many ways the most damaging of all emotions. The sense of inferiority, shame, failure, rejection, and guilt are almost indistinguishable from one another. Each of these emotions suggests a sense of worthlessness.

This generalized sense of guilt, real or false, generates tremendous anxiety. Whether one has violated social mores, religious principles, laws of the state, or one's own ethical and moral standards, the superego condemns the violation. The condemnation is carried out by an intricate mechanism which results in a feeling of apprehension, anxiety, and tension in the organism. This is actually a wise and beneficial provision. It serves the same purpose as physical pain, which is a warning signal that something is wrong. When the situation is taken care of, the physical pain normally subsides. It has served its purpose. In the case of anxiety and consequent physical tension, when guilt has been resolved through confession, repentance, and a change of conduct, the anxiety should disappear. Unfortunately, in too many instances this is not the case. Millions of people continue to suffer pangs of remorse and generalized anxiety long after confession, repentance, and a change in conduct.

One form of self-punishment which guilt takes is physical illness. Guilt demands either confession or punishment. It is not God who makes this demand, but the inner judicial self. If a sense of forgiveness and consequent release is not experienced and if the outraged conscience continues to demand punishment, very often it will take the form of a physical symptom. Illness is employed as a means of this self-punishment. "The neurotic has to behave as though he were mastered by guilt, which the illness serves to punish, and so to relieve him,"[4] as Freud pointed out. It is not God, of course, who visits illness upon the individual, but the inexorable judicial system within which will settle for nothing less than forgiveness or punishment.

This subtle mechanism if often seen in children. Little Mary Lou had done something forbidden while her mother was in another part of the house. She had gotten into her mother's clothes closet and tried on several of her dresses. In the process she tripped in one of the dresses and tore it. Hastily she put the dress back, hoping that her mother would not discover it. The rest of the day Mary Lou was a brat. She was rebellious, disobedient, and generally offensive. Her mother warned her, yelled at her, and finally threatened her with punishment unless she settled down. But Mary Lou was anxiety-ridden and did not confess. Without being aware of it, she needed to be punished. Finally in exasperation over the little girl's impossible conduct her mother spanked her. There were screams of pain and rage, but in a few minutes Mary Lou was playing contentedly in her room. Her mother congratulated herself on applying the ancient adage, "Spare the rod and spoil the child," unaware that she had punished her daughter for something other than general brattiness. Mary Lou, without at all being aware of it, had "atoned" for her sin.

Guilt Demands Punishment

Charles was a fine young man but badly coordinated physically and emotionally ill-equipped to face life. In his late twenties he committed suicide. His mother, whom I knew well, felt a deep sense of loss and guilt. In her mind she had been responsible for his failure and for his having taken his own life. She could not discuss this deep sense of guilt. Had she been able to do so it is possible that she might have been able to discharge the enormous anxiety that developed as a result of her guilt feelings.

Within a month she was killed in an auto accident. No one else was seriously injured. There is no reason to believe that she had any conscious intention of taking her own life. She was not the sort of person who, had she intended to do so, would have planned an accident involving other people. Rather it appeared that at an unconscious level she experienced such a sense of guilt that she no longer felt any desire to live. Normally a careful driver, she was killed in an accident in which she was obviously at fault. The inexorable inner judge had pronounced judgment. She "paid the price" of her real or imagined guilt.

Generalized anxiety has reached such proportions

119

in the United States that the Food and Drug Administration has taken action to limit the number of tranquilizers a patient may secure on one prescription. According to an FDA official, the provision will prevent anyone from securing a refill of the two most used tranquilizers after six months. After that period of time a new prescription must be obtained from a doctor. He pointed out that millions of people are hooked on tranquilizers, some taking as many as thirty or more a day when three to four would be a normal dosage.

Mrs. America, a Junkie?

The assistant head of the vice squad of the Des Moines police department gave a group this profile of Mrs. America:

> She's a white, upper middle income housewife who drinks three cups of coffee in the morning to get going, and takes her Benzedrine (or equivalent) because at 120 pounds she'd like to weigh 110. She smokes two to three cigarettes during the nervous period of driving her children to school, and her husband to the commuter train.
>
> About 3:30 P.M. knowing that she will have to face the kids again, she takes her tranquilizers to calm her down. After picking up her husband at the train she has three martinis with him before dinner. After dinner and with the kids in bed they glue themselves to the boob tube with beer at their sides. Now it's time for sleep, and she takes her Seconal—a barbiturate—to sleep. Mrs. America is actually a junkie. She takes speed, tranquilizers, alcohol and barbiturates. Should she wonder why her son (or daughter) has been picked up for smoking marijuana?[5]

It would be patently unfair to convey the impression that only Mrs. America is a junkie. Men, no less than women, are operating under an enormous load of anxiety in our culture and use anxiety-alleviating drugs—alcohol and pills—as palliatives. There is some evidence, in the minds of many authorities, that alcohol addiction is a far greater menace to society than illicit drugs. Dr. A. Dudley Dennison says:

> Seventy-eight percent of men and 63 percent of women spend 16½ billion dollars annually on alcohol. This is twice as much as is spent on all welfare programs and religion combined. This produces, among other things, the 25,000 alcohol-related deaths on the highway, 28,000 deaths from cirrhosis of the liver and other causes, plus 9 million alcoholics and another estimated 10 million problem drinkers.
>
> If the headlines were to tell us tomorrow that three thousand young people died last year as the result of drug abuse the nation would be up in arms. However, there are an estimated 3,000 sleeping pill deaths each year, nearly all of them adults. Nine million pounds of barbiturates are manufactured each year for the American market, which is enough to give 25 doses to every man, woman and child in the country. This is the measure of the anxiety with which we live.[6]

Simply to be alive is to experience anxiety to some degree. Up to a certain level it is our friend. Without it we would be ambulatory vegetables. It is almost certain that every act, however small, is an effort to reduce anxiety or alleviate it in some way. Ordinarily anxiety is so slight that we may be unaware of it or experience it simply as a vague uneasiness which disappears as soon as we have taken the appropriate action. One of the most common manifestations of excessive anxiety is tension. It may reveal itself as tension headache, low back pains, generalized tightness throughout the body, with or without accompanying pain, or in a dozen different ways, often below the level of consciousness. Excessive fatigue is often experienced as the result of keeping anxiety below the level of awareness.

Unrealistic Expectations

Another main cause of chronic anxiety is unrealistic expectations, together with trying to meet deadlines.

The false belief that life should be one long succession of mildly euphoric experiences can produce anxiety. The hectic pursuit of happiness, which always seems to elude the frantic pursuer, generates enormous amounts of anxiety. Actually, the search for happiness is a false goal. In most lives genuinely happy experiences are relatively few and far between. But there are misguided individuals who feel cheated because they cannot experience a more or less continual state of blissful euphoria they have learned to expect.

The belief that marriage will bring unalloyed bliss is a remarkably long-lived myth of adolescence. It is partly the product of idealistic and unrealistic youth and partly the result of romantic movies, TV, and novels. In reality marriage is probably the most difficult of all relationships. A very good marriage can be most gratifying and fulfilling. A bad one can be shattering. But, of course, marriages don't fail; people do. There are no ideal marriages for the simple reason that there are no ideal people. Trying to work out a satisfactory marriage relationship and rear children (a complex task for which there is almost no training in our culture) can be the source of enormous anxiety.

To these anxiety-producing situations and relationships we can add some of the more obvious ones: keeping up appearances; meeting new people; performing on the job and trying to meet the expectations of an employer; attempting to meet our own expectations as humans, members of society, and members of the family; and the very real, though often unconscious, effort to meet the moral and spiritual requirements established by God.

As I have noted, anxiety begins at birth. Being precipitated into the world after the long peaceful months in the velvety warmth of the womb is a traumatic event. Ashley Montague, the anthropologist, discusses in *The Human Revolution* various theories having to do with the prolonged labor of a human mother. "Labor pains may average two hours in apes. In the human species labor generally lasts about fourteen hours with the first child, and some eight hours with later-born children. What can be the meaning of this long period of labor in the human species?"[7] Montague offers several possible explanations and then suggests rather tentatively the theory of Otto Rank, a colleague of Freud. "Prolonged labor is one of nature's ways of reinforcing the need to be appropriately anxious as a defense against dangerous situations when they arise." In other words, Rank is suggesting that the first gift of nature to the newborn child is a gigantic load of anxiety to prepare the infant for an anxiety-filled life ahead of him.

While there is no evidence to validate the theory, it is obvious that without the capacity for anxiety a human being would be without normal fear in the face of threat and devoid of concern for the future although planning ahead is one essential for survival. Thus, anxiety is a vitally important survival factor without which civilization would long ago have ceased to exist. But in excessive amounts it can either destroy us or make life miserable. A moderate degree of anxiety can cause us to be concerned for the rights of others. It creates appropriate concern when faced with decisions having to do with matters of ethics and morality.

Anxiety and Tension

Abnormal or neurotic anxiety, on the other hand, limits us in leading creative lives and causes us to expend psychic energy in conduct which may be contrary to our best interest. For instance, a couple whom I knew quite well experienced considerable tension in their marriage, as well as a great deal of unresolved conflict within themselves individually. They never faced either their marital or personal problems honestly but unconsciously sought to discharge their anxiety and consequent tension in an interesting but neurotic way. In the eight years I knew them, during which time he changed jobs four or five times, they bought and sold

123

nine homes in one community. In each new home they worked diligently to decorate it just the way they wanted it. Having done so, they then became dissatisfied and began looking for another house more to their liking. They lost money on eight of the nine houses when they sold them, but they were able to rationalize this in each instance. Their inner anxiety was so great that they found a way, unconsciously, to displace it onto another supposed cause of unhappiness—the inability to find just the right house.

The average retired man, who has no satisfying hobbies or other suitable activity to occupy his time, dies within two years of retirement. For most of a lifetime he has had a reason for existence. A reasonable amount of anxiety got him out of bed every morning and to his job. A suitable degree of inner tension, essential for the proper functioning of the physical and psychic organism, had been generated by his daily schedule. Upon retirement, to which he looked forward with so much anticipation, there is nothing to challenge him. He really has nothing to live for, and so he dies.

Insecurity can be either creative or destructive. In one sense there is no absolute security in this life. The future is always relatively uncertain. A multitude of variables can disrupt one's most carefully laid plans. It is, in a sense, this very insecurity which makes the game worth playing. Even in the games we humans invent, we always incorporate in them some element of uncertainty. It is no fun if the outcome is always a foregone conclusion, if we always know who is going to win. So life's uncertainties and built-in insecurities, exasperating as they can be at times, pose the challenge that makes it worthwhile. But there are amorphous insecurities so generalized that they lie in a tangled mass in the unconscious mind. These nameless insecurities, of which most people are not consciously aware, generate anxiety which must be discharged in some way. Some of the ways we choose are harmless; some, mildly destructive; and others, ultimately disastrous, depending upon the amount of psychic energy expended upon them.

For instance, the typical rigid fundamentalist is usually a very insecure, anxiety-ridden person. Far from trying to discourage him, or attempting to show him the folly of his fanaticism, I would advocate that he cling to his rigid orthodoxy as long as he needs it. He is at that point in his spiritual and emotional development where he *needs* that particular authoritarian brand of theology. If it gives him a sense of security to know without any shadow of a doubt that Adam and Eve were historical persons, I would not argue with him. For one thing, I have no way of knowing that he is wrong. I feel no need to subscribe to his barren and, to me, loveless orthodoxy, but I can understand his great anxiety which requires an authoritarian religion. It is with considerable humility that I look back upon a period in my own life when just such a rigid, authoritarian orthodoxy seemed to satisfy some unnamed anxious need.

Onward and Upward

Rigidity of belief, such as doctrinal rigidity, says Robert S. De Ropp, "is a way of avoiding anxiety caused by uncertainty. In spite of all our insistence about wanting to be free, most of us in some degree still feel a very strong need to be told what to believe and what to think. This is an unconscious need. In general the masses want to be told what to do, what to wear, to think and to believe. This automatically saves them from the effort involved in thinking for themselves. This also applies to religious belief because once an individual has discovered a 'faith' he will protect this with an enormous and passionate intensity, because if any doubt about the validity of his belief creeps in, it can create enormous anxiety."[8]

In *The Supreme Identity,* Alan Watts describes some of the common manifestations of anxiety: "The psychology of 'bigger and better,' of the record smasher, the money maker, the imperialist, the speed maniac, the time saver, and the religious fanatic . . . has not the faintest idea of when or where to stop. He knows only that he wants more and more and more of the same—more speed, more cash, more power, more territory, more concerts, more thrills. He wants to possess infinity, whereas the man of sensibility asks only to be possessed by infinity." When possessed by ultimate reality, "man is at last free to love things and people for themselves rather than for what he can get out of them. Free from anxiety and impatience he can concentrate on the creation of quality rather than quantity. Free from the compulsion to deserve eternal life by piling up merits, he can love people with their benefit in mind rather than his own salvation."[9]

The nervous, frenetic pace of Western civilization is anxiety-producing. The benefits of our civilization are also the tangible results of a creative anxiety. It would be wrong to label our Western civilization all good and Oriental cultures as all bad. The ideal probably lies somewhere in between or rather in a mixture of Oriental patience and mysticism and Western drive and creativity. These two traits could ideally be incorporated into one personality. Jesus seems to have experienced periods of intense activity. As Mark records, they were so busy with the crowds seeking to get near him that "they had no leisure even to eat" (Mark 6:31, RSV). Then there were times when he felt a need to be alone for meditation and prayer. This alternation is something that is lacking in most lives. We tend to get caught up in a hectic round of activities which consume virtually every waking hour. Many people have reported the common experience of sensing a need for a quiet time during the day and then discovering that for some reason they avoid it or cannot find time for it. The probable truth is that meditation and reflection are so foreign to our frantic temperaments that to quiet down and indulge in silent meditation actually creates a vague and disconcerting anxiety. There comes the feeling, as I have experienced it, that "I ought to be doing something." It is only by an act of the will that I can take myself by the back of the neck and sit down for a period of quiet reflection. When I do, I always find it either restful or productive of some insight or that it tends to recharge my psychic batteries. What perverse streak is it, then, that causes us at times, to avoid the quiet time?

If Christ himself withdrew into the mountains to pray, the most ardent muscular Christian cannot use the world's urgent need for bread as an excuse for the indefinite postponement of spiritual contemplation. Yet in most Christian churches the average sermon is a stirring call to action directed to people, who, having no spiritual repose, are not ready to be spiritually awake.[10]

Chapter 9

ANXIETY AND GUILT

> *He who has too light a conscience must*
> *needs learn the fear of God. He whose con-*
> *science is too severe should think on the*
> *grace of God.*
>
> GERMAINE ST. CLOUD

"I committed a murder," she told me, "and for years
I've felt a need to find someone with whom I could
safely share this terrible guilt." She was a very attractive woman in her thirties. I had observed her in the
opening days of the retreat. She appeared to be a
happy, outgoing person. Now as she shared her guilty
past, I was looking at a miserably unhappy individual.
The anguish of an old, guilty secret showed clearly on
her face.

"Apparently you sensed that I wouldn't judge you,"
I said.

"Yes, I'm sure of that. I've needed to confess this to
someone for so long, and I guess this is the time." She
paused and seemed uncertain as to how to begin. "You
see, I was going with this young man. He wasn't the
sort of person I would have wanted to marry, but I did
enjoy him. Then it happened. I got pregnant. I was
very young, and of course I was terrified. My parents
insisted that I get an abortion. They seemed concerned

only over the fact that there might be a scandal. I felt terribly guilty about the idea of taking the life that was beginning to be formed in me, but my parents insisted, and so I went ahead with the abortion. I've felt guilty ever since. I committed a murder, and I haven't had a moment's peace in all these years."

In recent years the attitude of many people about abortion has changed radically. However, even if I had felt led to try, I could not have lessened her feeling of guilt over the abortion. Accordingly I dealt with the guilt as she perceived it and proceeded to give her absolution. I asked the woman to bow her head and close her eyes. Then I quoted a half-dozen of the promises concerning God's forgiveness of sin. After that I affirmed that inasmuch as she had repented and confessed, she was fully and completely and forever forgiven. I explained the meaning of the cross—Christ's demonstration of God's eternal love, which embodies forgiveness and cleansing.

She breathed deeply and relaxed. It was as though the burden of years of self-accusations had been lifted. Later she told me that the guilt had been so great that she had not been able to live a fulfilling life. The anxiety generated by guilt had used up so much of her psychic energy that she had very little left with which to cope with life.

Guilt is probably the most destructive of all emotions. It is a form of self-hate. The virtuous part of the personality accuses the guilty portion. This accusation is hurled by the conscience with such vehemence, in some instances, that the entire organism suffers. The usual result is that an all-pervasive, generalized anxiety is felt. In some persons it manifests itself as depression. In others it expresses itself as an inferiority complex, for in one sense guilt and inferiority are the same emotion.

Guilt and Fear

Rejection, inferiority, shame, failure, and guilt all register the same on the spiritual and emotional nature.

The generalized feeling is one of worthlessness, as though we felt ourselves to be worth less than before or less worthy than others.

Guilt is one of the greatest fear inducers. Whether the guilt is real or false, the inevitable result in a typical human being is fear. This is recognized in the New Testament in a passage which is usually quoted only in part. Most Christians are familiar with the statement that "perfect love casts out fear." The complete passage reads, "There is no fear in love, but perfect love casts out fear. *For fear has to do with punishment,* and he who fears is not perfected in love" (1 John 4:18, RSV, italics mine). The part which concerns us here is the section which asserts that "fear has to do with punishment." There is a fundamental anxiety which derives its power from the fear of being punished. As children we were punished, in one way or another, when we disobeyed or displeased our parents. Thus there is a kind of conditioned response which promotes the feeling: I have done wrong; I deserve to be punished.

If we have acted contrary to our ethical or moral standards, the inner judicial system is activated and declares: You must be punished. This is a kind of psychic warning bell which continues to sound its alarm until one of two things takes place: either we are forgiven, or we must be punished. This is not the edict of God but of our own conscience. If we do not feel forgiven, the warning bell continues to ring in the form of anxiety. This anxiety can then be allayed by some form of punishment. God does not punish, but the inexorable inner judicial system does. There are numerous ways by which we punish ourselves, or rather by which the "accusatory self" punishes the "sinful self." Depending upon various factors, one may become accident prone, failure prone, sickness prone, bad-judgment prone, or simply go into depression.

The oft-used admonition, "Let your conscience be your guide," is wretched advice. The conscience does not come from God imprinted with the Ten Commandments, the Sermon on the Mount, and the traffic laws of your particular state, together with social customs. Conscience comes with only two words stamped on it: Do Right! Then our parents and our particular culture teach us what is right and what is wrong, all the way from murder, robbery, and traffic violations to such social customs as to which fork to use.

Failure in any realm—moral, social, marital, financial—registers on the emotional structure as guilt. For instance, a woman whose marriage fails usually feels a sense of existential guilt, regardless of who was to blame, just as a man whose business fails may feel what can only be described as guilt. Thus failure, which registers as guilt, produces anxiety. Such anxiety is not simply a vague and mildly troublesome emotion tugging at consciousness. In many instances it can prove devastating or even fatal.

Failure, Guilt, and Anxiety

A friend of mine had a business failure. He struggled for five years or more to avoid bankruptcy. During that time I observed a growing tension and anxiety which was understandable under the circumstances. One day he invited me to lunch. It is not easy for most men to share emotions. He laughed rather apologetically and said, "You know, sometimes during this struggle to keep my business afloat I've wondered if I were losing my mind." I decoded the mesage to read: "Help!" He was not so constituted as to ask for help directly, but in occasional luncheon meetings thereafter I offered such indirect help as I felt he could accept. He eventually did go into bankruptcy, spent some time in a hospital recuperating physically and emotionally, and then launched an entirely different career. He has been successful in his new venture, but he still recalls vividly the terrific anxiety generated by the knowledge that he had failed. I can detect no difference in his emotional reaction to that experience and the reaction of someone who is experiencing feelings of guilt.

Some people grow up in an environment which produces intense scrupulosity—another term for an overactive conscience. Such persons feel guilty on almost all counts. Others who are reared in a family environment where moral judgment is less severe are usually devoid of the overactive conscience and are often more healthy emotionally. There are still others whose moral and spiritual indoctrination is so lax that they become psychopathic deviates or sociopaths—people entirely devoid of moral values.

The very small child learns that "No, No!" refers to something forbidden. A bit later he learns the meaning of *good* and *bad* and may ask, "Have I been good today, mommy?" Sometime later he learns the meaning of right and wrong. He discovers, too, that a violation of a "No, No" or to be bad or wrong may bring either punishment or rejection. Thus is conscience formed. Threats such as "Just wait until your father gets home" or "God will punish you" are among the more damaging types of correction which can be used by a parent. The hours until daddy gets home may seem an eternity to the child. The waiting alone is usually far more punishment than the action warrants. The threat that "God will punish you" or in its lesser form, "God doesn't like you when you do that," is on a par with, "I'll have to tell the policeman to come and get you." All such threats are confessions of failure on the part of the parent. To generate excessive anxiety with threats which may or may not be carried out is to lay the groundwork for emotional problems in later life.

Some types of religion, especially the hell-fire and damnation type of fundamentalism, can produce an enormous amount of needless anxiety. If a child is exposed to this *and* a punitive home environment, enormous damage can be done to the personality. A young woman said: "I was reared by parents who, terrified of hell, couldn't afford to do anything unright, think anything unnice, feel anything un-Christian. Saddled with superior intellects (father had a Ph.D. and

133

mother, an M.D.), somehow they had to accommodate reason, blind faith, and a hideous fear in the same skulls. What precarious lives people can live." A guilt complex is usually the product of either harsh and judgmental parents or a combination of such parents and a judgmental religious background. Punitive parents usually justify their behavior by saying to themselves that they are determined to have "good" children. Very often parents disagree on the severity of punishment meted out to their children. Almost invariably I discover that the punitive parent had the same kind of parents and the less-harsh parent had parents who were more permissive.

The Guilt Complex and Anxiety

A guilt complex is seldom related to actual guilt. While such a person may be as guilty as the rest of the human race, his excessive sense of guilt is more of an all-pervasive sense of being wrong, bad, evil, sinful. Judging himself as guilty, he feels a need to fail or to be punished. The masochistic or self-punishing type of person may unconsciously marry someone who will provide the punishment.

An attractive and highly intelligent woman told me in a counseling session that she had been married five times, in each case to a man who turned out to be an alcoholic. She was searching for some reason within herself for choosing such men. Eventually we discovered the source. She had deep feelings of unworthiness, coupled with a kind but dominant personality. Accordingly she sought out men who were passive-aggressive. Her somewhat dominant nature was unconsciously attracted to passive men, and her deep feelings of unworthiness and guilt (mostly false) led her unwittingly to men who were aggressive and violent when drunk. Thus she had unconsciously satisfied two neurotic needs. She was horrified when she discovered the inner mechanism which prompted her to repeat the same mistake five times.

134

I knew a man over a period of years who was accident prone and failure prone. He had an almost unbelievable number of accidents and failed in business three times. Ethically and morally he was above the average. As a Christian he earnestly sought to do the will of God. Yet his harsh early home environment had been such that he had a very deep sense of inferiority. An inferiority complex and a guilt complex can produce the same results in the emotional structure. Both create undue anxiety and suggest a "need" to be punished.

A woman once told me of her terrible fear of God. I said, "An abnormal fear of God usually results from a sense of guilt. Whether your guilt is real or false I have no way of knowing."

She then shared with me the fact that her parents were harsh and punitive and that she had grown up in an extremely judgmental religious atmosphere. The combination had produced in her a guilt complex of staggering proportions. Her fear of God was on a par with the fear she had felt toward her father. We dealt with numerous things about which she felt guilty. None of them seemed to be of sufficient magnitude to account for her terrible fear of God; but when she had shared everything about which she felt guilty, I prayed a prayer of affirmation, in which she was assured of God's forgiveness. When I had finished, she still looked a little uncertain. So I said, "I know all about the things that made you feel guilty, and I do not think less of you. In fact I like you better for your beautiful honesty and humility."

"Is God like that, accepting us even when we're guilty?" she asked.

"Of course. I accept you and do not feel critical of you. God does that to an infinite degree."

She was able to accept that at a deep emotional level. When I next saw her, she appeared to have changed radically. There was a look of relaxation and peace about her that I had not seen before. She said, "Since

135

I have come to have a friendly relationship with God, everything is changed. Now I see more clearly that God is like Jesus, just as accepting and forgiving. I knew it in my head before, but now I have an entirely different attitude toward God. The difference in me has changed our home. I thought my husband and children were the problem. Now I know it was mainly in me. My husband and kids have changed in reaction to me."

Factors That Create an Anxiety Neurosis

This is as good a place as any to share the fact that for many years I had an anxiety neurosis and was unaware of it. Perhaps it would not be too great an over-simplification to define a neurosis as a "strong over-reaction." For instance, a car backfires in the street outside your home. If you look startled momentarily and jump slightly, that would be normal. If, however, you habitually jumped out of your chair every time a car backfired, that would be a neurotic behavior pattern—an overreaction. My excessive anxiety, or anxiety neurosis, manifested itself as extreme tension. I knew that I was tense, but having lived with it all my life I had grown accustomed to it. For all I knew, other people felt much the same way.

Whether we are anxious because we are tense or tense because we are anxious matters very little. The two seem to be inextricably interwoven. Psychosomatic ailments took their toll. None were very great, but like most anxiety neuroses mine produced a series of "floating symptoms"—mildly aggravating but never serious. I was vaguely aware that the physical symptoms were a warning signal that there were malfunctions in my personality. However, I was too busy being busy—a part of the neurosis—to pay much attention to the problem.

Now that most of the excessive anxiety has disappeared I can view it more objectively. What was the source of that inner tension and anxiety that had driven me for so long? Apparently it had its origin in three factors. First, there was a father who had the same anxiety neurosis. There is no one to blame. His father had something of the same sort, and perhaps *his* father before him. At any rate, I seemed to have absorbed some of my anxiety by osmosis. Children usually pick up, before the age of six the emotional "feeling tones" of one or both parents. A second factor was the judgmental atmosphere in which I grew up. Both at home and at church I felt the same judgment and criticism. I had failed. I did nothing right. God was going to judge me. As a child I was never sure that God loved me. I felt much more strongly that he was a frowning God writing down my sins in a book. A third source, related to the second, was a deep sense of guilt. My guilt was both real and false. There was a long period as a child when I lied incessantly. I didn't know at that age that children lie in order to defend themselves from criticism or attack.

For a time I stole everything that wasn't nailed down. I could not have known then that if a child keeps on stealing after he reaches the age of knowing "what is mine and what is thine" he is taking things as a substitute for love. So I felt inordinately guilty. There were other things, too, about which I felt guilty. Most of the guilt was false, but of course I didn't know that. I felt guilty about everything except going to Sunday school and taking a bath.

How Anxiety Neurosis Spreads Out

Since, as observed earlier, "Fear has to do with punishment," I developed an abnormal fear very early. The fear of God and his judgment, not to mention more immediate parental judgment, spread over to other areas: fear of people, of the dark, of speaking, of falling, and others. Fear produces abnormal tension. This suggests being pulled between two forces, in my case between guilt and forgiveness, right and wrong, sin and salvation, good and bad. Anxiety, as a natural concomitant, took its toll. The voice of the church and parent now became my own, and I felt a need to produce, to

137

succeed, to be busy, to compensate, to atone. This, of course, adds up to being a compulsive worker. The one kind thing that can be said about a compulsive worker is that he gets a great deal of work done. (Since compulsiveness originates in guilt feelings, compulsive people need all the kindness they can get. They have usually had all of the criticism and judgment they can handle.)

It seems to me that most of my life I ran. "Run and get me the hammer." "Run and ask your father . . ." "Run and help your mother." "Run and tell your sister . . ." "Run and answer the phone," and on and on and on. The faster I ran the more approval I got, or the less criticism. So I kept on running as an adult in order to win the approval of my own inner judicial system. To stop and rest created considerable anxiety. Never sit down. Do something. Keep busy. The devil has work for idle hands. Get a move on. Don't be lazy. That old parent tape with those and hundreds of similar phrases is still playing in my head.

Knowing where it all started doesn't solve the problem, but it helps in that one can sense that there is no need to blame oneself or one's parents; they did their best. They too were damaged by their parents. *There is no one to blame*—least of all ourselves. Self-blame compounds the guilt and makes things worse. There is guilt *only* if we fail to do something about it. Thus guilt, both real and false, generates anxiety. To relieve the anxiety one needs to discover at a deep level the limitless love and forgiveness of God. Many years after I knew about the love of God and had proclaimed it earnestly, the anxiety neurosis was still at work, for the source of the anxiety was much older than my knowledge about the love of God.

Some people respond to his love much more readily than others. We are all damaged to varying degrees. We respond in different ways, at different times, for no two of us are alike. Some of us are able to secure relief from excessive anxiety only after long and arduous efforts to get intellectual concepts down into the emotional structure. It is one thing to *know* about the love and forgiveness of God, but quite another to believe it and accept it at the deepest level of one's being. It helped me to affirm over and over to my own soul, many times a day and for many months, that God loved me, forgave me, and accepted me, and that as a result I could love and forgive and accept myself. Just as the anxiety had been created layer by layer, day by day, over a period of many years, the sense of forgiveness needed to be affirmed over and over until it displaced the condemnatory, judgmental, critical messages of the past.

A man said, "I told God, 'Lord, I committed the same sin again.' And God said, 'Really? What sin was that?' " God cannot remember a sin which he has forgiven. "I will remember your sins no more against you" is part and parcel of the love and acceptance of God as revealed in Christ.

Chapter 10

ANXIETY AND LOVE

> *Life is what happens to you while you're making plans for the future.*
>
> ANONYMOUS

Three of us were having a cup of coffee after a ministers' retreat session. Jim, a very quiet individual in his early thirties, had said little. "Jim," I said, "I seem to pick up in your voice some ancient sadness, perhaps as old as you are. What happened?" Very slowly and quietly he told his story.

"My father was an alcoholic, which wasn't the least of his deficiencies. He worked away from home most of the time; so I didn't see much of him. He didn't send enough money home to support the family; so my mother worked the bars as a cocktail waitress, and in other ways I didn't seem to understand.

"When I was seven, she had a baby. Everyone understood that it wasn't my father's child, and there was quite a lot of talk about it. The baby was given up for adoption. My father, incidentally, supplemented his income by pimping and bootlegging.

"When I was about eight, my parents were divorced, and I went to live with my father. The house was only partially furnished. The floors and walls were completely bare. Bottles and beer cans were everywhere. I was always glad when some prostitute came to live with us for a while because then the place would be cleaned up and there'd be someone there when I came home from school. There was a whole succession of prostitutes who came in from time to time to live with us. They became my surrogate mothers.

"By the time I was thirteen, I was drinking heavily. I guess it was around that age that I was first arrested for drunkenness. There were many other times too. When I was about fifteen, I was thrown into a cell to sober up, and the police went to look for my father. They found him in a bar, drunk. They put him into the same cell with me. When he sobered up, he took off his metal-studded belt and beat me until I passed out."

This was all related slowly in Jim's rather unemotional voice as though he were giving a weather report. I sensed that the hurt was too deep to admit fully into awareness.

"When I was seventeen, I was in jail again on a drunk charge. A Young Life worker happened to hear about me and came to bail me out. He told me in very simple terms that God loved me and that I must accept his love. To the best of my ability I did. Then he introduced me to a local church. They became my family. They made me feel wanted and loved. That summer the Young Life worker raised the money, somehow, to take me to a week-long Young Life Conference in Canada. That was another turning point. There I came to understand more about the love of God, and I accepted it more completely.

"I think I can still quote almost verbatim something that one of the speakers said, quoting Tillich. It was this: 'You are accepted; you are accepted! Accepted by one whose name you do not know. Do not try to find it now; perhaps you will find it later. Do not do anything, perform anything, intend anything. Simply accept the fact that you are accepted.'

"When I graduated from high school, I decided to go

to college. I had $142 in the bank which I had saved and about $30 in my pocket. I worked my way through college and somewhere along the way decided to enter the ministry. My wife and I both worked, of course. Sometimes I'd stay out of school for a quarter and work, then go back. Finally I graduated. Now I'm the pastor of a church. That's about all, I guess."

Jim's eyes, as he told his story, matched his voice. They showed something of the hurt and sadness of the past. When he had finished, I was aware of an enormous wave of compassion for a lonely, battered little boy, reared by an alcoholic father and a succession of prostitutes. And I felt, too, deep gratitude that a young man had taken the time and trouble to go to the jail and display such loving concern for a seventeen-year-old boy he had never seen before. Consider the enormous amount of anxiety generated in a child growing up in such an environment. An absence of love inevitably creates great anxiety in children. He was saved from certain ruin by the man who visited him in prison and by the warmth and friendship of the church members whom he remembers with deep gratitude.

Life's Hurts Are in the Present

The events of childhood are in the past, but the hurts are in the present. I could sense them in Jim even before he told his story. The course of his life was changed, but he will always bear the emotional scars of those early years. In a sense they have become redemptive scars, for they have rendered him infinitely more compassionate. As a minister he is capable of a far greater depth of understanding and empathy because of what he has experienced.

Perhaps this is the meaning of the Apostle Paul's statement: "Give thanks in all circumstances" (1 Thess. 5:18, RSV). That does not mean, as I see it, that we are to thank God *for* every hardship or disaster, rather to thank him for the fact that *in* every experience we can

143

discover unexpected dividends, either for ourselves or for others. Elsewhere Paul wrote that the hardships he had undergone—shipwreck, hunger, privation, beatings —had "really served to advance the gospel" (Phil. 1.12, RSV). "Perfect love casts out fear." Or, in other words, the greater our love, the more our fear and anxiety will be dissipated. In Jim's case, the love manifested by the Young Life worker and by the people at the church tended to cast out or diminish the enormous anxiety generated by an unbelievably harsh childhood environment.

In every marriage relationship there is almost inevitably a certain amount of anxiety. As the glow of the first days or months gives way to the mundane realities of daily living, the discovery is made that there are certain incompatibilities which had never been suspected during courtship. In my counseling I see again and again how much anxiety is generated as the result of a couple's inability to communicate or relate satisfactorily. One man, married for over forty years, shared his sense of frustration: "It isn't that we don't have a good marriage; we do. At least it's a good one by current standards. We don't fight and seldom argue. We lead a respectable, comfortable life."

"In that case," I asked, "what is it that bothers you?"

"The fact that our relationship is so superficial. Long ago I learned that my wife is very threatened by the idea of revealing her deep feelings."

"Do you attempt to share yours with her?"

"I did a few times, and I got a polite, slightly guarded response. It was obvious that it was going to be a one-way street, and I can't communicate with someone on that basis. So I gave up. Good grief! I can communicate more deeply with a dozen other people, both men and women. I can share at a deep feeling level with them."

"Does that satisfy your needs?"

"It helps, but in a way I feel guilty sharing feelings— especially with another woman—that I would like to

144

share with my wife. Besides I am afraid of getting emotionally involved with some other woman, and that can happen, you know, if you share deeply. Being understood is very close to a feeling of love, and I don't want to destroy my marriage, mediocre as it is."

"So, what do you do when someone, male or female, opens up and invites communication at a deep feeling level?"

"With a man I can share. I share laughter and tears. I can't do that with my wife. It would rattle her cage—the tears, I mean. I laugh more with my friends by far than I do at home."

"What about the women who invite you to share with them?"

"I usually cut them off, as much as I would like to share my deeper feelings with them. I don't want a woman getting into my emotions. It makes me vulnerable. I could be vulnerable with my wife if she could reciprocate. But she's so afraid of her deep feelings that she'd slash her wrists before she'd let me see any of her inner weaknesses and her deep feelings—as if I weren't aware of them already."

"So, where does that leave you?"

"Just where I was, I've spent forty years and more this way, and I can live it out. Just sharing this frustration has been helpful. But there's a lot more. I'll probably be back to dump more of it later on."

"One more question: Are you angry at your wife because you feel frustrated?"

"I never thought of it before. I suppose I am, but I conceal it pretty well. I guess it shows up in the form of my being distracted and often very quiet. Incidentally, I just realized something. I start to reveal some feelings, and then I get the usual guarded, polite, response, and I get angry. Then I resolve never again—never!—to let my feelings show around my wife. But I keep doing it and go on resolving to talk only about trivia. About nine-tenths of the time I succeed. So we settle for trivia, minutiae."

145

"Your's isn't a bad marriage then, just mildly frustrating?"

"Yes, that's about it; unfulfilling would be a better word. My wife feels unfulfilled, too, because she can't help but pick up some of my frustration or anger or whatever it is. And then she doesn't feel loved. I can't fake it."

Publicly Adored, Privately Endured

That describes one of the *better* marriages. The thousands that fall on the lower portion of the scale suffer enormous anxiety. I recall a woman who spent a considerable amount of time in a mental institution. When she was eligible for release, I put her in a group and saw her privately for several years. Not until I got to know her husband did I begin to suspect the source of the deep anxiety which had resulted in her mental breakdown.

She always praised her husband highly and expressed the deepest love for him. After meeting him I attributed her excessive admiration to a lack of discrimination and a vast need for love, together with a very deprived childhood. With various kinds of therapy she managed to maintain her emotional equilibrium for several years, but from time to time she would manifest certain alarming symptoms. Then her beloved husband died. At the funeral she was among the most composed. Not a tear was shed, but she kept up her comments about his wonderful qualities. Information gleaned at the funeral, however, seemed to warrant my earlier suspicions. The husband was impossible. He was universally regarded as boorish, loud, offensive, and as a person to be avoided at all costs. No one had a kind or complimentary thing to say about him. I had feared that his wife would feel devastated after his death, for she had known deep loss and heartbreak as a child and later in life as well.

Instead, she began to brighten up. She laughed more often and was much gayer. She began to dress more colorfully. Within a month or two of her husband's death she embarked upon an entirely new venture. She was, in short, a new woman. The source of her anxiety neurosis and mental illness had been a husband whom she publicly adored and privately endured at great cost to her mental stability.

"It is quite clear that between love and understanding there is a very close link," writes Dr. Paul Tournier. "He who loves understands, and he who understands loves. . . . A man needs to feel very deeply loved in order to share an intimate secret charged with emotion. . . . He may tell of some dreamlike ideal to which he holds very deeply . . . an inner call, a sense of mission which he is to fulfill in the world. It seemed that he could never dare speak of it to another. He feared that it would appear ridiculous or vain, and yet, suddenly, without his knowing why, the rapport with another has become such that he uncovers his long-hidden secret.

"A thousand fears keep us in check. First of all there is the fear of breaking down, of crying. There is especially the fear that the other will not sense the tremendous importance with which this memory or feeling is charged. How painful it is when such a difficult sharing falls flat, upon ears either preoccupied or mocking, ears in any case that do not sense the significance of what we're saying."[1]

Women, who are usually much more at home with their emotions, perhaps feel this more strongly than most men, for men in our culture learn that there is something shameful about revealing feelings. A woman may feel a sense of painful rejection if her feelings are brushed aside or ignored. Men more often hide the secret feeling, and if it is revealed and rejected, conceal the hurt beneath a facade of indifference or anger. Men pay a penalty for thus hiding their feelings. Their life span is some eight years shorter than that of women, who are more in touch with their feelings. Children and young people also experience the anxiety occasioned by a lack of understanding and love.

Listening As an Act of Love

Love is not just an emotion. It is an action, or at least it can express itself in actions. And listening is an act of love! If there is any one sin of which parents are more guilty than others, it is failure to listen. Children are admonished, scolded, advised, lectured, threatened, and yelled at; or, if the parents are highly controlled individuals, the child is treated coolly, but when emotions are muted, the child picks up the feeling tones just as strongly as if he or she had been screamed at.

Children can be irritating with their incessant demands for attention. They often want to talk about something important to them at the most inconvenient times. Parents have rights, too; yet if a child—of whatever age—receives five or ten negative responses for every friendly or positive word of affirmation, the foundation is being laid for trouble later on.

I was in the home of a man one evening discussing some matters of considerable importance. Four or five times during the course of our conversation his five-year-old daughter came into the room to ask or tell him something. It was not an attention-getting device but a legitimate need to confer with her daddy. My reaction, after the third or fourth interruption, was one of irritation. I wondered whether the mother could not have met the child's needs; but a bit later, when the little girl crawled up into her father's lap and sat there blissfully happy, I sensed that the need for the moment was to relate to daddy, not mommy. She was going through the Oedipal stage, and daddy was the most important person in the whole world. I shifted gears emotionally and found my mild irritation vanishing as I sensed how wise the father was in listening to his little girl *at the time* she needed to communicate with him.

Anxiety is generated if we are not heard, if no one listens. The very refusal to listen with interest is a way of saying, "You don't matter. I don't care enough about you to listen to your needs." A great deal of emphasis is put upon training people to communicate, which has the connotation of *talking*. We need to stress also the vast importance of *listening*. In the art of communication there are three very important fundamentals:

"Tell me all about it" is one appropriate response when we sense that the other has something to say. It might be phrased various ways, depending upon circumstances, such as, "What happened?" The expression on one's face and the tone of voice need to be congruent with the spoken words. A bored expression and a flat, uninterested tone of voice can belie the utterance. People often say that they feel hypocritical voicing an interest they do not feel. The answer to that is that *it is never hypocritical or phony to act appropriately*. Feelings tend to follow actions. In time your feelings will catch up with your actions if you act appropriately.

Listen! Listening is a genuine art, much neglected. One may not be passionately concerned about what is being said, but if it is of interest to the speaker, then as an act of friendship, love, or mere politeness, one needs to listen with intensity.

I once watched a world-famous man of great charm and ability at a social function. He had been cornered by a compulsive talker, a man who evidenced little culture or intelligence. For a considerable length of time the little man held forth on some topic. I was near enough to hear part of the conversation which seemed to me unutterably boring. But the listener never took his eyes from the face of the other. It was one of the most gracious things I had witnessed in a long time—an act of Christian love and consideration. I have a half-dozen devices for disentangling myself from time-wasters and compulsive talkers. The listener in this case displayed far more patience and forbearance than I could have.

Husbands and wives seldom listen to each other with deep interest unless they have made a studied effort to learn the art. Almost nothing is as interesting to the listener as to the one relating some story or event. It *is*

149

difficult to listen with interest to something which doesn't seem terribly important or vital. But, in any relationship, since listening is an act of love, it doesn't really matter whether one is interested or not. If I love or care about the other, I will listen whether I find the conversation interesting or not.

Validate the feelings of the other. This involves something like, "Yes, I can see why you'd feel that way." Perhaps you can't fully, but if you had the emotional wiring of the other and possessed that person's environmental background, education, and personality, you would undoubtedly feel precisely as the other person does. Some other responses might be, "You must feel very happy over the good news," or "That experience must really have shaken you pretty deeply," or "That must have been a rough experience. What happened after that?" Among the worst things that can be said, especially in a family setting, would be: "That was a dumb thing to do!" "Why didn't you tell them off?" "If I'd been in your place I'd have told them. . . ." "For heaven's sake, why would you get so upset over such a little thing?" "You shouldn't feel that way."

Advice-giving Is Not Listening

The problem-solving male, and to a somewhat lesser degree the practically minded female, will often come up with some solutions: "Now here's what you need to do. . . ." Usually, however, at this point the other person is not asking for advice or seeking solutions. Just now what is needed is a *listener.* Often we don't know what we really feel until we hear what we have to say. Feelings can be sorted out later, solutions, worked out the next day. For the moment the thing to do is to listen without letting one's eyes glaze over or wander to the TV set or the newspaper headlines.

A wife and mother in such a situation, listening to her husband, needs to decide on priorities. Little Jimmy's plea for attention may conceivably be lower on the priority scale than the husband's need to relate a harrowing event at the office. But a comment such as, "Tell me more later, dear, it's time for dinner now," may well shut off communication for some time. Is it not possible that serving dinner ten minutes later could be an act of love if the postponement is due to listening with rapt attention to one's husband? A husband's favorite TV program can often be sacrificed profitably to a wife's need to communicate. One can check priorities and values. Which is more important—having dinner on time, watching a TV program, or having a warm, understanding relationship? No one knows how many husbands have strayed because at home they received a cool impersonal, "Yes, dear, that's very interesting, but I have to do something just now. Later, perhaps . . ." At the office or elsewhere there are any number of women who are anxious to listen with bated breath and unwavering gaze to his every word. Perhaps, if he decides to divorce his uncomprehending wife who takes him for granted and marry this breathless and loving woman who listens so eagerly, he may discover that she is not such a good listener *after* marriage.

A woman reported that her dull, stodgy, uncommunicative husband bored her to tears. She became enamored of a married man who, too, felt trapped in his marriage. After months of delightful communication with him and some surreptitious evenings together, she had half decided to break up her marriage and marry this utterly charming man. Then one day she chanced to overhear the man's wife talking about her husband. He was described as boring, uncommunicative, unimaginative, a poor lover, and in fact a total loss. The listening woman said, "Her description of her husband sounded so much like my own that I decided to stay married and try to work out a better relationship." It could be just possible, she said, that part of the fault lay in her.

After dealing with several thousand married couples, I have seen ample evidence to warrant a broad generalization: men often seem unaware of the importance

151

to women of what men term "little things"; and women, by and large, seem oblivious of the fact that men can be as sensitive as women. This lack of understanding can create a great deal of anxiety in male-female relationships.

Passive Husband, Dominant Wife

At a seminar where I was working with twenty men, a rather passive, sensitive, and somewhat depressed young man told of his unhappy marriage. His wife had been on her own since the age of thirteen. "She doesn't seem to need me. She's self-reliant and fears her emotions. She won't talk about feelings. We have little or no communication."

"Has she ever told you what her needs are or indicated how you can express love to her?" he was asked.

"Yes, but it's kind of silly. She seems to derive some absurd kind of pleasure from having me mop the kitchen floor occasionally or help her wash dishes, a lot of those little things. To me, love is expressed by being able to communicate at a deep level."

The group sought to show him that his wife's needs were legitimate. Her home was an extension of her personality, and to neglect it was the same as neglecting her; to show it attention and concern was the same as showing it to her. He looked puzzled but agreed to ask her to list the specific ways, large or small, in which he could express love. "If that's the only way she can accept love, or even one of the ways, I guess I can try," he said. But as he described his wife's reactions, I sensed that she probably understood him as poorly as he did her. She was aggressive, competent, and self-reliant. He was quite passive, deeply sensitive, and easily hurt. It seemed highly probable that she, who had battled her way through life, could not comprehend how deeply hurt he could be by something which would not disturb her.

A woman said to her husband of thirty years, "I never realized before how sensitive you are." She was genuinely amazed. It had taken her thirty years to discover his secret.

He made no comment then; but to a friend he said, later, "If it took her all that time to learn a simple thing like that about me, I am not going to make myself any more vulnerable than I am. I'll keep my façade up. I share myself at a feeling level with others, both men and women, where I am confident of not being destroyed, or rejected, or looked at cooly as if I were a bit odd for having such feelings."

Anxiety, of course, is created in excessive amounts when we repress our deeper feelings or suppress strong emotions. In moderate amounts anxiety is a survival factor and a vital part of one's personality; in excessive amounts it can cause any number of physical or emotional problems. A very composed man sits calmly smoking his pipe. No one would ever suspect that he is excessively tense and anxious unless one's gaze fell on his foot which is in constant, vigorous, motion.

A placid-faced woman with a sweet smile carries on a quiet conversation in the same room. I am the only one who knows that she is in a state of deep depression, resulting from an almost unbearable anxiety. I could scarcely have guessed it when she came in for her first counseling session. She masked it beautifully. Only her eyes betrayed her, where fear lurked. She and her husband had been inseparable. It had been a symbiotic relationship: he outgoing, independent, daring; she very dependent and quite willing to let him make virtually every decision. She did not even know how to fill in a check stub. When he died suddenly, it threw her into a panic, with feelings of anxiety, loneliness, and a vast sense of desolation. It required three or four years for her to recover, not from the grief, but to achieve a sense of her own identity and learn how to make a life for herself after thrity years of being a passive, dependent satellite to a dominant husband.

Chapter 11

ANXIETY, SEX AND ANGER

> *Egotism is the result of trying to prove that you are worthwhile after having sunk into self-hate. Loving yourself will dissipate your egotism; you will feel no need to prove you are superior.*
>
> THADDEUS GOLAS

There were twenty ministers at a retreat which I was leading at a beautiful mountain resort. One of the men became ill during a session and was driven to a physician in a nearby town. He spent the rest of the day in bed. The next day, feeling somewhat better, he asked if he could talk with me. He began rather hesitantly. "I have begun to wonder if this physical symptom of mine might be related to an event which took place thirty years ago."

"Tell me about it."

"Well, when I was attending the university, I was engaged to the young woman whom I later married. We had occasional sexual intercourse, and she became pregnant. I felt terribly guilty. I told the university chaplain about it, and he tried to help me see that it was not the end of the world. We were married, but for the last thirty years I have continued to feel guilty. I've confessed it over and over to God, and I suppose I've confessed to a dozen different persons, but there's never been any sense of relief from the guilt. My stern religious background has given me a strict conscience. So, now I've come to wonder if this guilt complex of mine has something to do with the physical symptom which shows up periodically."

He was sharing this with a deep sense of shame. There was an air of sadness or depression as he talked. I could feel only deep compassion for a man who had lived under the lash of a thirty-year guilt complex.

I asked, "What leads you to suspect that the physical symptom is related to your guilt feelings?"

"Well, not too long ago my grown son—the one conceived out of wedlock—came to visit us. I had told him about it long before, and he had tried to assure me that it was all right. He just said, 'I'm here, dad, and that's all that matters.' But as we set out for a game of tennis, I became ill and had to go back home. Another time, not long afterwards, I was on my way to church one Sunday morning when the illness struck me again. I had planned to preach about repentance. I had to return home when the same physical symptom hit me. And now, a third time I have experienced it, here."

"What happened here that could have triggered the old guilt feelings?" I asked.

"I think it was the letter that went out giving details of this retreat. We were asked to be prepared 'to be honest.'"

"How often," I asked him, "have you confessed this event?"

"Many times. I keep telling people about it in the hope that it will relieve me and help me forgive myself. I know all about the forgiveness of God, but I have never been able to forgive myself."

"All right, let's start with one important point: I am the end of the line. I am the last person you are to share this with. The next step is to recognize something you have somehow missed. Do you know the difference between a marriage and a wedding?"

"They take place at the same time. They are the same thing."

156

"Not necessarily. When you and the girl to whom you were engaged committed yourselves to each other, in God's sight you were married. You gave yourselves to each other when you agreed to spend the rest of your lives together. That moment, in God's sight and in actuality, you were married. You legalized it later when the wedding ceremony took place, as a way of publicly notifying the community that you were beginning life together. There was a mistake in that it has caused untold anguish in the form of unresolved guilt. But a sin, no. In saying this I am not recommending premarital sex. I neither condone nor condemn. I am simply saying that you have labored under a terrible misapprehension."

Then I gave him absolution. I quoted every Scripture I could recall concerning God's love and his acceptance. I assured him of God's forgiveness, and then finally I said, "My friend, I scarcely knew you when you came to my room. Right now I have some strong feelings about you. I feel for you. I like you. I admire your honesty and humility, and more important, I love you." We stood up, and I embraced him.

Before he left, I shared with him a formula for achieving a self-forgiveness which many have found helpful. I told him to repeat this prayer of affirmation ten times a day for ninety days, as a means of assuring his inner emotional structure of what he knew in his head: God forgives me, and I now forgive myself; God accepts me, and I now accept myself; God loves me, and I will love myself properly. I told him that within three months he could achieve a complete sense of self-forgiveness and release from self-accusation, but I added that old habit patterns tend to reassert themselves. He would need to use the affirmation prayer again from time to time whenever the old doubts and guilts began to reappear.

My friend was the victim of a very common problem: a mixture of real and false guilt, and inability to forgive himself despite the intellectual knowledge that

God had accepted and forgiven him. Fear of punishment for what he had felt was an enormous sin led him to anticipate, unconsciously, some form of future punishment. This created great anxiety. Since no punishment was forthcoming, his inner judicial system had proceeded to punish him with an emotionally induced illness.

Our Strongest Drives

Since sex and anger are the two strongest human drives, it is understandable that these two emotions cause the most guilt, and hence the most anxiety. Some people have been able to handle the sex drive satisfactorily, but in some degree, according to many authorities, most people have mild to severe anxiety in the area of sex.

Masters and Johnson of St. Louis have probably done the most extensive and effective work in the field of human sexuality. They report that in at least 50 percent of marriages sex relations are a disaster. In another 25 percent sex relations and attitudes leave something to be desired. Since the sex drive is so strong, it has many possibilities for damage to society and the individual. Accordingly, in virtually all cultures, both primitive and modern, strict taboos and regulations have been established concerning this most potent of human drives. The violation of these taboos normally creates a sense of guilt and thus anxiety.

Another factor having to do with the creation of anxiety is that in primitive society, for thousands of years, a boy of fifteen or sixteen and a girl of thirteen or fourteen would be married according to tribal custom. The onset of puberty was the signal that the person was ready to begin establishing a home and rearing a family. In the close-knit tribal culture, parents and other relatives and friends would help prepare the girl and her young husband for the task of parenthood. In our modern culture, with the more or less standard requirement of a high school diploma and preferably a college degree, marriage is often postponed until the couple is in their early twenties, perhaps nine to fourteen years after they have become physically able to undertake sexual activities. During all the years between puberty and marriage, the strongest drive a human being experiences is seeking expression. This God-given emotion can create enormous anxiety. The sex drive is saying go, and parents and society—not to mention financial realities—are saying wait!

Another less-recognized factor is the way a typical infant is treated by mother or surrogate mothers. At a very early age the infant begins to explore his world. He clutches at toys, plays with his toes, and finally in his all-out effort to discover this fascinating world, his hands find the genital area. It is almost an automatic reaction for many mothers to remove or slap the hands and to say, "No, No!" Dealing with a somewhat older child, a mother may say, "Don't touch yourself down there. That's dirty!" The child thus comes by a very natural process to equate the sexual area with "dirty" or at least "forbidden." This all takes place in most instances before the age of memory when the emotional structure is very sensitive to all in-puts.

In dealing with a young husband who was virtually impotent, I discussed the possibility that this hand-slapping technique might have been used with him, together with later negative impressions from mother. He said: "Why, yes, I'm sure that happened to me. I watched my mother do that precise thing to my little sister who was then about two or three years old. Mother had a terrible sex hang-up, and I'm confident that I must have been treated much as my sister was. So, *that's* the origin of my enormous anxiety about the whole subject of sex!"

The Source of Our Excessive Guilt

While it is probably true that the Puritans introduced a considerable amount of sex guilt into our culture, there is a much older and stronger source. In an effort to avoid the immorality of the Romans, with their food and sex orgies, the early Christians stressed the spiritual and aesthetic aspect of life. "Sensuality" and sexuality" were more or less equated with "sin." To *enjoy* the sense of sight, taste, smell, hearing, and touch was to "live for the flesh." This was deemed carnal and therefore evil.

Jone's *Moral Theology*[1] devotes forty-four pages to a discussion of the various categories of sin, of which thirty-two pages, in fine print, are devoted to sexual sins. This left only twelve of his forty-four pages with which to deal with lying, murder, greed, avarice, covetousness, self-righteousness, lust, and all the rest of the spiritual and physical sins. The author's preoccupation with sexual sins was not unusual for a Catholic theologian of that period.

The Church Fathers virtually equated sex with sin and seemingly identified sexual feelings with lust. The sexual organs, they admitted, were pure since they were creations of God, but they saw the attraction of the sexes as something fundamentally evil. The Christian attitude toward sex, both Catholic and Protestant, in some degree has been influenced by the writings of Augustine and other early church leaders. Augustine, for example, wrote of "ideal sexuality" as it might have been before the fall. Speaking of the sex organs he wrote:

> Those members, like the rest, would be moved by the command of his will, and the husband would be mingled with the loins of the wife, without the seductive stimulus of passion, with calmness of mind and with no corruption of the innocence of the body, because the wild heat of passion would not activate those parts of the body, but, as would be proper, a voluntary control would employ them. Thus it would have been possible to inject the semen into the womb through the female genitalia as innocently as the menstrual flow is now ejected.[2]

If the pendulum has now swung to the opposite extreme so that perverted aspects of human sexuality are exhibited in movies and on the stage, this must be recognized for just what it is: an excessive and destructive reaction to certain false concepts. Neither extreme is productive of emotional and spiritual growth.

There is often a strange reluctance on the part of many people to discuss sexuality. In a minister's Yokefellow group to which I belonged for several years, I said at one session: "Fellows, we've talked about almost everything under the sun except the subject of sex. This morning let's share our feelings about that topic." There was a lengthy silence, then a young pastor shared his feelings of guilt over what he called lust. He had experienced great feelings of guilt and anxiety over the matter for years and felt relieved at being able to share this with an accepting group. It proved to be a helpful session, for it turned out that he had been equating physical attraction with lust.

"Do you intend to act on your physical impulses?" I asked.

"Good heavens, no!" he replied. "But I always thought that to look at a person of the opposite sex, as it says in the New Testament, is the same as committing adultery."

"You've made a tragic mistake," I said. "It says that to *look with lust* is equivalent to adultery, but I define lust as desire plus *intent*, and you indicated that you have no intent of ever carrying out any of the vagrant thoughts that enter your mind unbidden. Therefore you are innocent."

"And to think that all these years I've been condemning myself for committing a sin when it wasn't a sin at all! What a relief."

Christian or Pharisaical?

In the area of sex, marriage, and divorce, it seems to me that many Christians have been as judgmental as the Pharisees who flung a woman at Jesus' feet, accusing her of adultery. He said to her, as recorded by John, "Neither do I condemn you; go, and do not sin again" (John 8:3-11, RSV).

A physician in my community secured a divorce. He had been a member of the vestry of his church until that time. Several years later, desiring to remarry, his minister refused to perform the wedding ceremony, as he was not permitted to do so under church law. I performed the ceremony, whereupon he was accepted back into the church with open arms, as was his new wife. He said to me, "I find it little short of amazing that my own church, to which I have belonged for over thirty years, could not countenance a divorce and remarriage, but I am still a member in good standing and presumably still eligible to be a member of the vestry. How do you explain that?"

"I don't explain it," I said. "I just wonder whether we are not often more like the Pharisees than we are like Jesus."

Considerable anxiety is generated in a vast number of people by the subject of human sexuality. Feeling guilty over being sexual beings and over having the normal sex drive, many unmarried persons feel vaguely guilty or anxious over the unfulfilled sex drive. It is not only the Christians reared in a rigid and moralistic church and family setting who tend to feel guilty. I have discovered that many people with little or no religious background often feel just as guilty, having been reared in a home environment which treated sex as something one just doesn't talk about. And because the sex drive is so powerful, when it is ignored, denied, or treated as something shameful, great anxiety results.

A woman with no religious background, but with a faint knowledge of the Genesis story, said to me: "Wasn't it for sexual sin that Adam and Eve were thrown out of the Garden of Eden?"

"It is not so recorded," I said, "On the contrary God had earlier told them to 'be fruitful and multiply, and replenish the earth.' This would presumably suggest normal sex activity."

"Good grief, I never knew that! You mean God actually *commanded* them to—well . . . to . . ."

"Yes, he seems to have commanded them to have sexual relations, to procreate after their kind. I cannot imagine any other way by which Adam and Eve could have had children."

"My! It's good to know that God placed his seal of approval upon sexual activity. I've always thought of it as something rather shameful, at least to be used solely to produce children," she said.

"Look at it this way," I said. "God has given us the five senses. Among them is the sense of taste. To eat gluttonously, to live primarily for the sense of taste, would be to deny the other senses and ignore the spiritual side of our natures. But surely God meant us to *enjoy* the taste of a good steak, or ice cream, or anything else that we enjoy eating. Isn't it likely that since he gave us this enormous sex drive and linked it up with erogenous zones of the body he intended us to enjoy physical love, just as one enjoys a good banquet, or a great symphony, or the sight of a magnificent sunset? These are all sensuous experiences. Don't identify sensuality solely with sex. It is sensuous to enjoy great music, good art, good cooking, and expensive perfume. We are physical, sensual beings, as well as immortal, spiritual beings. Don't deny either part of your nature."

Anger and Anxiety

The other powerful emotion which can create considerable anxiety is anger. Perhaps only second in strength to the sex drive, anger is basically a survival factor. It is a God-given instinct to prepare one for defense or attack, whichever seems appropriate. An animal can express anger and, when the emergency passes, appear amiable and relaxed. Animals do not normally seem equipped to carry a grudge. They appear to possess an inner mechanism which permits them to express the fear or anger, act on it, and then revert to their normal mood. And of course they do not feel guilty about expressing anger.

In our culture the mother of a young child usually feels highly complimented when someone says of her offspring, "He's such a *good* child," meaning that he never does anything to cause the mother any added effort. He may conceivably be a blob of unimaginative protoplasm. He may have learned early in life that he could win mother's love and approval, and the cooing admiration of other mothers, by smiling inoffensively and burying any negative feelings. Children learn very early to adapt, to manipulate, to do whatever seems appropriate to survive and bask in mommy's love. If for some reason the quiet, inoffensive, compliant trick doesn't work, he can always try the aggressive bit, kicking, screaming, and hitting. *That* will get her attention!

A child may learn early in life that no form of anger is ever acceptable, that he is never to use the word *hate*. The supreme virtue, he finds, is to be "good." Unable to express any negative emotions he will usually grow into an adult who is afraid of his anger. He may, depending upon various factors, be a very passive individual or passive-aggressive. Having been conditioned by a parental tape to repress his anger, he may be completely unaware that he has a normal load of aggressiveness. Unable to express it appropriately he may suffer from asthma, arthritis, ulcers, ulcerative colitis, migraine headaches, neurodermatitis (a troublesome skin irritation often diagnosed as eczema), infections of the upper respiratory tract, or any of a score of other symptoms.

A man once shared with me the fact that he had what might be called a fairly good marriage, except that communication was limited to peripheral and totally mundane matters. "I'm as much to blame as my wife, I expect," he told me. "I have difficulty expressing much anger, or any negative emotion what-

164

ever for that matter. I find it very difficult to tell her when she's bugging me."

"How does she irritate you?"

"Well, she's a natural born lecturer and advice-giver. She loves to inform, to teach, to instruct, to come up with tidbits of information which will help her compensate for her inferiority complex. It doesn't show except in the ways she compensates for it."

"That strikes you as something very difficult to handle?"

"No, it doesn't except that I've listened to it for about forty years, and I'm tired of repressing, or suppressing, my anger. If I blew up every time she assumes the lecture stance, I'd be yelling at her all the time. I am not wired up to operate that way. I prefer peace and harmony, so I normally shut up and disappear."

"You mean retreat?"

"I prefer to think of it as disappearing."

"You cop out, in other words."

"I don't like that term, but I guess I do. I don't like to hurt her feelings."

"What happens when you have been able to confront her about this, or anything else that is an irritant?"

"She usually gets huffy and wants to argue the point. Then she denies that she does those things. Finally as a last resort, like a very patient school teacher with a slow learner, she points out some of my defects. My feeling at that point is to say, 'The hell with it,' and disappear—both physically and verbally. I find myself spending more time away from home, partly to have as little contact with her as possible. I simply refuse always to be attacking her about something that would seem minor, except that it's a gross irritant."

"Do you think you can live with it?" I asked.

"I have all these years."

"Any emotional or physical symptoms?"

"Yeah. A mild depression which may last for a few days when I 'disappear.' And now that you mention it,

I have had a whole raft of minor physical symptoms. If it isn't one, it's another. I know, down deep, it's my buried anger."

"Anything I can do?"

"No," he said thoughtfully. "You've listened while I blew my cork. That's all I needed, I guess."

"Would you like to learn how to confront her, or at least share your feelings?"

"No! I've learned to live with it."

Suppressed Anger and Anxiety

Anxiety is generated by not finding a suitable way of expressing anger or irritation. There are three basic ways to deal with anger and many other emotions. Anger may be *suppressed, repressed,* or *expressed.* To *suppress* it means to be aware of the emotion but to "sit on it" because it may be inappropriate to express it at the moment. It may be *expressed* directly or indirectly, tactfully or otherwise. In terms of mental health this is probably the most effective way of handling anger.

Unfortunately it is not always appropriate to express a negative emotion. The anger may be felt toward the boss, and to express it might conceivably result in being fired. Some individuals go through life spewing their anger uninhibitedly upon everyone. They learned early in life that one way to be secure is to control the environment. They play the game of uproar. Family, friends, and associates learn to fear them. They may have a certain amount of security, but usually their relationships are short-lived or very unsatisfactory.

The "blasters" who intimidate everyone around them in order to remain in control are far from being healthy emotionally. They are actually out of touch with their deeper emotions. Their blasting is produced by an inner sadistic rage which is "leaking" a form of hostility. It does not mean that they are aware of their feelings. The blaster, without knowing it consciously, has three motives: First, he is vaguely aware that by inducing fear in those about him he feels safer. Second, he is basically sadistic and enjoys seeing others suffer. Third, he is unwittingly blasting in order to avoid tender emotions which he equates with weakness. Thus, in order to avoid feeling weak, he must terrorize those about him. He does so, not out of strength, but out of weakness.

The most damaging way of handling anger is to *repress* it. Since this is done unconsciously, one normally has little if any control over the process. It is usually learned early in life. Many very angry people become quite placid and complacent, having buried the anger below the level of awareness. Sometimes they suffer the penalty of repression, which is a physical or emotional symptom, often of severe proportions.

Every normal human being experiences the emotion of anger. A person who cannot *feel* anger under *any* circumstances is repressing it. Jesus became angry on more than one occasion. One who cannot feel anger over gross injustice, or cruelty, or when under unprovoked attack is burying his emotions. Somewhere along the line he will pay a price for it in terms of emotional or physical symptoms. There are people who are more placid, more sanguine in temperament, than the average. These may be less easily aroused, than, for instance, someone who is easily provoked and has difficulty in controlling his emotions.

When Are We to "Turn the Other Cheek"?

Jesus taught that when provoked we are to "turn the other cheek." It is evident that he did not intend this to be applied under all circumstances. When attacked by the Pharisees, he defended himself. He "looked upon them with anger" on another occasion. He cleansed the temple, evicting a host of haggling merchants who polluted the outer temple area. When he faced the mob, however, with their chorus of "Crucify him!" he turned the other cheek, refusing to defend himself.

167

How can one know when to "be angry and sin not," as the New Testament advocates, and when to "turn the other cheek"? One may "lose or use" his temper. To *lose* it means to lose control of it, to be out of control emotionally. This is seldom a very creative response. Usually it results in more rancor than before and seldom resolves the initial problem. To *use* one's anger is, as in the case of Jesus' cleansing of the temple, to utilize the full extent of one's rage for the accomplishing of a worthy goal.

I was on a bus some years ago on the way to San Francisco. Four service men in the rear began a ribald conversation. Talking loudly enough to be heard by everyone on the bus, they became more and more profane and obscene. There were several women and children on the bus. I went forward and asked the bus driver to quiet the men as they were disturbing and offending the other passengers. He shook his head.

I am not given to this sort of thing as a common practice, but after a few minutes I heard myself shout to the offending soldiers, "Stop that talk! There will be no more of that on this bus!" Suddenly I realized that I might be in for a lot of trouble. People had been known to be beaten up on local buses. Martyrdom holds no great attraction for me. But to my surprise a great silence descended on the bus. The four men subsided and did not utter another word. A woman with a small child just ahead of me turned, smiled, and said, "Thanks." Suddenly I realized that I was not just irritated. I was very, very angry. And if I had not been that angry, I could never have asserted myself. Perhaps in a sense that is one function of anger: to enable us to overcome our natural reluctance to be other than pleasing and quiet and "nice" when the situation warrants it.

The Gunnysack Technique

One of the most harmful devices we can employ is to "gunnysack" our anger. A gunnysacker is one who carries an invisible bag over his shoulder and puts in tidbits of anger hour by hour, day after day. When the sack is filled and someone irritates him, however slightly, he erupts with unreasoning anger and dumps the whole load on the poor victim, who then asks in bewilderment, "What was *that* all about?" The gunnysacker, if he is at all aware of what he has been doing, might reply: "Sorry about that. I just dumped on you a load of anger I've been accumulating for my wife, my boss, and for a friend who let me down. You just happened to be the one who triggered the entire load. It's really not your fault at all." The gunnysacker seldom if ever responds that way, however. He is usually unaware—at least at the time—of what he has done.

One young man with an explosive temper which erupted at the slightest provocation once told me that he kept praying, "O Lord, I lost my temper again. Help me to restrain myself." I said, "I think you're praying about the wrong thing. You would do better to ask God to help you find out why you are so angry and at whom you are really angry." My suggestion fell on deaf ears. A few years later he came to see me about an unreasoning phobia which was driving him half crazy. He was praying that God would relieve him of the phobia. Again I said, "I think you are praying about the wrong thing. Ask God to help you discover the *source* of the phobia." Again my counsel was rejected. Ultimately his wife divorced him because, as she told me, "His probia drove *me* crazy. I didn't want to spend the rest of my life living with a man driven out of his mind with a phobia."

Underneath any unreasoning anger or fear there is always another, deeper cause. Using one or more of the methods described in the last chapter, it is possible to discover the roots of whatever it is that is causing inappropriate reactions.

Chapter 12

RELEASE—METHODS AND MEANS

> *Whether in the intellectual pursuits of science or in the mystical pursuits of the spirit, the light beckons ahead and the purpose surging in our nature responds.*
>
> SIR ARTHUR EDDINGTON
> Physicist, Astronomer

Never in the history of mankind have there been so many choices. The very proliferation of options makes for confusion and anxiety. In purchasing a new car the buyer confronts hundreds of models. In life-styles, tranquillizers, architectural plans, religion (there are over two hundred different Christian denominations and many different religions), vacation plans, frozen and packaged foods—in every area of life there are today a fantastic number of choices.

Millions of young people (and some not so young) have been caught up in a craze for things both ancient and modern—from astrology, which has been kicking around for some thousands of years, to Zen Buddhism, which is fairly ancient. Hare Krishna has attracted some adherents, as have a number of "Perfect Masters" from India. Seventy percent of more than 1750 daily newspapers in the United States, with forty million daily readers, carry horoscope columns with such gems as, "Aquarius (Jan. 21 to Feb. 19). Handle all obligations conscientiously and derive fine benefits therefrom. Do something thoughtful for mate and be more cooperative." Presumably this wisdom would not apply to one born a month earlier or later. More than ten thousand full-time and one hundred seventy-five thousand part-time astrologers practice in this country. Shakespeare, who took a dim view of astrology, has one of his characters say: "The fault, dear Brutus, is not in our stars, but in ourselves, that we are underlings." But many still search the stars for answers to life's basic questions.

There are many paths to God, though there is but one God. The search for answers is in reality a search for God, by whatever name. It is a longing for security, for peace, for a lessening of the existential anxiety which pervades the whole world. Dr. Werner von Braun of NASA, in an unpublished paper, wrote: "Whereas all other living beings seem to find their places in the natural order, and fulfill their role in life with a kind of calm acceptance, man exhibits confusion. Why the anxiety? Why the storm and stress? Man really seems to be the only living thing uncertain of his role in the universe; and in his uncertainty he has been calling since time immemorial upon the stars and the universe for salvation, and for answers to his eternal question: Who am I? Why am I here?"

With my whole heart I wish it were easy, that there might be found one answer for all people—one religion to which everyone could respond; one therapy which would provide release for all emotional problems; one pill which would cure all physical diseases; one simple answer to the problem of our existence. But of course this is simplistic and childish. We do not all enjoy the same foods, or dress exactly alike, or read the same books, or watch the same TV programs. We are different. We are not "wired up" the same way emotionally and do not respond emotionally and spiritually to the same rituals, or music, or literature or flower arrangements or architecture. We are *different* and respond to different methods, ideologies, and systems. This is all right, for no two persons were ever exactly alike in appearance or temperament or constitution. Hence the need for an eclectic approach to spiritual and emotional needs.

Christ Is the Answer

A recently converted college student, anxious to witness to his new-found faith, entered his classroom early every morning and wrote on the chalkboard: "Christ is the answer." After a week or two someone wrote under it: "Yes, but what's the question?" The assertion that Christ is the answer can be either a dreary cliché or a profound truth, depending upon various factors.

The Charismatic Movement

A woman whom I came to know quite well spent several years as a member of a group I was leading. During that time she underwent a number of severe crises—divorce, illness, financial difficulties, and an emotional disability which rendered her unable to hold down a full-time job which she needed very much. During the time she was in the group a number of others made significant progress in their emotional and spiritual growth. Evelyn just barely managed to hold herself together with the group's help. Week by week she reported on her current difficulties. I could perceive some growth but nothing significant. In time she joined another group interested in the charismatic movement. Within six months or so she was able to secure and hold down a full-time job for the first time. In some ways it was her most important breakthrough. She had desperately needed her Yokefellow group during her time of crisis, but the charismatic experience apparently provided the additional "something" she sorely needed.

I have not been involved in the charismatic movement, sometimes referred to as the "tongues movement," though that is only a part of the experience.

But I do not in the slightest deprecate it. There is ample evidence that it has been a power for good in the lives of millions of people. If in some instances divisiveness has resulted over the issue, this need not be considered fatal. There was divisiveness over the same issue in the church at Corinth. The problem seems to lie, not in the "gift of the spirit," but with the contentiousness of people both in and out of the movement. There is ample evidence that for many people the charismatic experience has been the means of measurable spiritual and emotional growth. For some it has provided solutions to life's problems hitherto insoluble.

Hypnotism

To my knowledge no qualified psychologist or psychiatrist suggests hypnotism as a "cure." It is used in some instances by qualified therapists as a means of dredging up deeply buried material from childhood. It has also been used with occasional success in reconditioning a conditioned response, in helping to break certain habits such as smoking or overeating. However, not everyone is a good subject, and usually a great deal of reinforcement is necessary. In other words, hypnotism is not a one-shot deal, and it does not always work.

Psychoanalysis

English psychiatrist H. J. Eysenck claims that his studies show no difference in the recovery rate of patients receiving psychoanalytic treatment, and patients who were given no treatment whatever. In other words, whether a person did or did not receive psychoanalysis made no difference.

Another study revealed that among patients suffering from emotional problems, 42 percent improved under psychoanalysis; 64 percent showed improvement when receiving standard psychiatric treatment (talk therapy), and of those receiving no treatment whatever, 72 percent showed improvement.

Another discouraging factor is the cost. A full course of psychoanalysis can take from three to five years, preferably on a daily basis, and may cost anywhere from ten to thirty thousand dollars.

Small groups

Under many different names and using varied approaches, small groups have proliferated in the past few years. Numerous studies of such groups have turned up a variety of both negative and positive findings. Perhaps one of the most significant findings is that a typical therapy group, of whatever type, may be no more effective than the leader. Other things being equal, it seems that many untrained leaders do *even better* than clinically trained personnel. Dr. Werner Mendel, professor of psychiatry at the University of Southern California, set up a three-part experiment. One group of patients was led by trained psychiatrists and the other top staff members at the hospital. A second group was led by a less adequately trained crew of psychotherapists and clinical psychologists. The third group was ministered to by persons having no formal training in therapy. *The groups led by the untrained individuals fared best.* Those treated by the most highly trained staff members showed the least improvement. Mendel was so surprised by the results that he repeated the experiment with different patients and other leaders. The results were the same. *The nonprofessional leaders did best.*

This is not to suggest that just any person is qualified to be a group leader; yet virtually every church in America utilizes relatively untrained persons to teach Bible school classes. To these individuals we entrust the spiritual well-being of millions of children, young people, and adults without a second thought!

At a large mental institution on the West Coast one of the psychiatrists told me that they had seventy-six groups meeting several times a week. They did not have sufficient trained personnel and called upon office workers and other untrained personnel to convene the meetings. There was one group without a leader, and a staff member suggested that the truck driver be asked to lead it. "At least he can convene the group and ask them what they want to talk about," someone suggested. The staff watched Joe, the truck driver, rather carefully. At first it was to make sure that he would make no serious mistakes. Later, I was told, he was not just watched but studied because a larger percentage of his group was dismissed from the institution than from any other group; and a smaller number of his released patients returned to the hospital than from other groups. "We studied him to see how he did it," I was told.

"What did you find out?" I asked.

"Well, we discovered three things. First, he loved those people and cared about them. They sensed it, and it made a big difference. Second, he was strong and took no foolishness from them. Third, he had a native common sense and some basic insight into human nature. These three things outweighed all of the formal psychiatric training the rest of us had received."

According to Dr. Jim Bebout, of the Write Institute in Berkeley, California, "Professional therapists do not usually do well as leaders." His findings emerge from a massive study supported by the National Institute of Mental Health. Studies of lay-led groups indicated, according to Dr. Bebout, that "such groups tend to improve self-satisfaction, self-reliance, and lessen anxiety, loneliness, alienation and social inhibition."

Dr. Karl Menninger writes in *The Vital Balance*, "Psychiatry continues to expand. It is no longer the private esoteric wisdom of a few traditions. Psychiatry is a discipline served by doctors, psychologists, lawyers, judges, clergymen and welfare workers."[1]

Psychiatrist Jerome D. Frank, a faculty member at John Hopkins School of Medicine who holds a Ph.D. in psychology and an M.D. from Harvard University, believes that a person with no training at all can be just as successful a clinician as a psychiatrist. He holds that "the therapist's personal qualities may have more to do with his success than his training in a particular method." Dr. Frank is the co-author of *Group Psychotherapy* and *Sanity and Survival* and presumably qualified to speak authoritatively on the subject.

Megavitamin Therapy

There are some people who suffer from subclinical metabolic disturbances or from serious vitamin deficiencies which have been undetected. They are unable to function normally because they are chemically not up to par.

A woman approached me after a retreat on the East Coast, just as I was leaving to catch my plane. She said that their son had been in a mental institution for nine years and that no form of therapy had been productive. I said, "Just on the off-chance that he may be suffering from hypoglycemia [low blood sugar], you might try megavitamin therapy. It's inexpensive and involves the use of a few vitamins in high dosages, none of which causes side effects." I promised to send her some material about it. She wrote some months later to report that their son had been discharged from the hospital, had secured a job, and was normal for the first time in nine years. They had tried the megavitamin approach with phenomenal results.

Obviously there are many causes of emotional illness, and perhaps in only certain cases would this approach prove effective. But there is ample clinical evidence that low blood sugar (which can be diagnosed with a five-hour glucose tolerance test) can result in many forms of physical and emotional illness. There is a considerable body of evidence indicating that problem drinkers can benefit from a combination of the megavitamin therapy, a high protein-low carbohydrate diet, and a group experience. Recent reports from a San Francisco researcher have indicated that some hyperactive children tended to improve when all sugar was withdrawn from the diet. This is further evidence of the link between emotions and diet.

Reconditioning the Conditioned Response

This is sometimes called the "paradoxical intention" approach, an elaboration of William James's principle of "act as if" or "do the thing you fear to do." In the case of an extremely shy person it is certainly more likely to be effective than "talk therapy." For instance, an excessively timid person walks up to a stranger at church, or at a social function, and introduces himself. Then he engages the stranger in conversation for a given length of time. He makes it his goal to seek out every occasion where he can practice. He must keep setting his goal higher each week: one stranger this week, two next week, three the next week, and so on. By acting as if he were not afraid, in time the old fear (a conditioned response) diminishes. Often the difficulty may be such that the subject may need a group, or a therapist, to whom he can report. The group or counselor can provide the required emotional support and guidance to help the individual maintain a sustained effort.

The term *paradoxical intention* describes the process: paradoxically one does intentionally the thing he fears to do. By repeating the feared action he is reconditioning the conditioned response. Pavlov demonstrated that it was possible to "erase" a conditioned response either as the result of intense fear or panic, or by repetitiously doing the precise opposite of the original action.

Meditation

Since the earliest days of Christianity, and with certain other religions even before that, meditation has been used as a means of achieving greater awareness of oneself, of spiritual reality, of the outer world, of God, and of one's fellow-man. There was a great revival of interest in mysticism during the fifteenth and sixteenth centuries. Many monks and Christians at large sought a new awareness of God through prayer and reflection. One classic dated from that general period is *The Cloud of Unknowing* by an unnamed monk. It is still published.

There is a current revival of interest in meditation. Whether by the term *Transcendental Meditation* or any other designation, the process of taking two fifteen- or twenty-minute periods a day for quiet reflection and meditation can be recommended for anyone. Erich Fromm, asked for a practical solution to the problem of living, replied, "The experience of stillness. You have to stop in order to change direction."

Ours is not a quiet or reflective age. The very atmosphere is tense and rushed. We tend to fill up every hour of every day. The only persons who are likely to investigate the ancient art of meditation are those who are (1) hurting very much, and thus highly motivated, (2) searching earnestly for some answers, or (3) are open to new dimensions of personal growth. Virtually anyone who really wants to can find the required time, despite all frenzied denials to the contrary.

A young wife and mother who belonged to one of our Yokefellow groups said to me: "At first I found it rather difficult to find the time or opportunity for the meditation suggested by our group. But since I had promised to try it for ninety days, I was determined to give it a try. There was no time during the day, what with one preschool youngster and another in school. So I decided to get up a half-hour earlier every morning for my reading and meditation. I got so much benefit from it that I stretched it to an hour."

"Don't you miss the sleep?" I asked.

"No, I find I don't need as much sleep as I did because I am much less tense and nervous."

Her husband interrupted at this point: "I notice that for the first time since we got married you aren't yelling at the kids when I come home."

"Right," she said, "and for the first time since we've

had kids, you aren't too tired to play with them when you come home from work. Your quiet time is paying off, too, isn't it?"

"Yeah, I guess it is. I hadn't thought of it, the way you put it, but I do have more energy now, come to think of it."

It is usually easier for many undisciplined people (which includes most of us to undertake this along with a group of like-minded persons. They tend to check up on each other good-naturedly, or, in their joint study of quiet time techniques, they tend to reinforce each other in the undertaking.

The fact that numerous East Indian religions promote the art of meditation has made the process suspect in the minds of some people. But one need not adopt an Eastern religion in order to derive benefit from a daily program of reflection and quiet. The Bible emphasizes the value of seeking this stillness: "In quietness and in trust you shall find your strength" (Isa. 30:15, RSV). "Be still, and know that I am God" (Psa. 46:10, RSV). The list of quotations could be extended indefinitely.

Retreats

There are probably more weekend retreats now being conducted under the auspices of religious organizations and movements of various kinds than at any other time in history. Among these are Faith at Work, which does an excellent job of conducting retreats in many sections of the country, the Lay Witness Movement, Yokefellows, and many others. And of course, churches by the thousands are encouraging their members to attend weekend retreats.

Among the nonreligious retreats, perhaps the best known is Esalen, in Northern California, where there is a year-round program involving many different types of psychological methods. Nationally and internationally known speakers lead not only weekend sessions there but many courses of longer duration. The founder of Esalen was quoted in *Life* magazine as saying that although approximately 95 percent of those participating in retreats report initially having received benefits, after a year only about 5 percent indicated that there had been any long-term results. Perhaps one reason for the somewhat discouraging report could be that many retreatants had expected that their lives would be changed as the result of a weekend or a month's experience at Esalen. It has taken us a long time to become the persons we are. Few of us are going to have ancient life patterns altered radically and permanently as the result of a weekend experience, *unless there is some kind of follow-up*.

People attending Faith at Work and Yokefellow conferences normally have their church activities to help reinforce any spiritual gains made at the retreat, and the same is true of the Lay Witness Movement and other similar church-oriented movements.

If the twelve who followed Jesus for three years, and who lived so intimately with him, could fail so dramatically at the end and reveal so little spiritual insight, it seems reasonable to assume that it can require somewhat more than a weekend experience to provide a radically changed life-situation or an altered personality.

Private Counseling

There are times when personal counseling seems indicated. One need not be facing a crisis of major proportions in order to benefit from the services of a marriage counselor or psychologist, and one need not be considered "sick" emotionally to consult a psychiatrist. The day is long past when a visit to a psychiatrist was tantamount to admitting that you were in bad shape mentally. Today millions of people see psychologists and psychiatrists in order to have the help of a trained, competent, objective person in resolving some personal situation. Everyone has a problem, lives with a problem, or is a problem. To resolve some of these problems it is often essential to secure professional help.

Primal or In-depth Therapy

It is as difficult to describe this type of therapy as to describe any other method or technique. However it is possible to explain some of the emotional, psychological, and spiritual aspects of the process. This type of approach has been in use for many years, under various names. A number of religiously oriented individuals have utilized a similar approach termed *the healing of memories*. Dr. Arthur Janov and Dr. Louis Casriel popularized the method within recent years and Janov coined the term *primal therapy*.

First let it be said that there is no one type of therapy which meets the needs of everyone. Human needs vary enormously. Primal therapy is not the solution for all the world's ills, nor is any other technique. However, there are some underlying assumptions which can well be examined:

There is nothing seriously wrong with any of us except "hurts," usually experienced in childhood. To be freed of the damaging emotional effects of such events or influences, the hurts must be relived with about as much emotional pain as when they were first experienced. In psychological terminology this is often referred to as "abreaction." In order to help an individual go back and relive these hurts, many of which are repressed, it is usually essential to regress the person to childhood. This is accomplished by a process called ageregression. The subject reexperiences the events of childhood, but at the same time is usually aware of where he is and what is transpiring around him. The subject is living in two "time worlds" simultaneously.

At least 99 percent of all that transpired prior to the age of four has been "forgotten" by the conscious mind and put in dead storage (the unconscious mind). Much of what happened *after* age four has also been forgotten. Many painful memories are repressed, together with material not essential for survival. Therefore it becomes necessary to go back and relive some of these experiences, to bring them to light, and to feel them with the same emotional intensity as the original event. This is normally done under the guidance of a skilled therapist in comfortable, safe surroundings. It would be wonderful if all of the ancient hurts of a lifetime could be reexperienced and dumped in an hour or two. Unfortunately, as with any other type of therapy, it may require considerable time, depending upon the number and extent of the primal "hurts." Some patients come in once a week for several months, on occasion, for a year or more. Others, depending on many factors, achieve excellent results in much less time. Some come in daily for a period of three weeks or more, setting aside a block of time for this purpose.

In competent hands, as with any other type of therapy, there are no harmful effects. The process often provides great relief for many people who, until undergoing this type of experience, were not even aware of what it was in the past that was causing so much difficulty. The term *in-depth therapy* is used by the therapists at the Burlingame Counseling Center, associated with the Yokefellow Center. As with any other approach, the skill and consideration of the therapist is of paramount importance. When carried out by sensitive, skillful therapists, the results are often dramatic.

Yokefellow Groups

Since 1957, Yokefellow groups have been conducted on the West Coast; and since 1959 this type of group has spread to all fifty states and several foreign countries. There are other Yokefellow Centers, primarily but not exclusively of the retreat type, in other parts of the country.

It is difficult to give a verbal description of a typical group, just as one could not give a meaningful description of a worship service or a thrilling theater performance. However, it is possible to outline briefly some of the ground rules, methods, and dividends. In general it could be said that a Yokefellow group aims at providing a new dimension in emotional and spiritual growth. Such a group, properly conducted, begins at the same point where Jesus often started: "What do you want me to do for you?" or, in other words, "Where are you hurting?" Jesus never began with some historical event in the remote past or with a theological doctrine to which one was to subscribe. *He started at the point of pain.* A Yokefellow group normally takes the same approach.

One need not be facing some monumental crisis in order to benefit from such a group. The need may not be the sharp stab of a crisis but the dull throb of frustration—the feeling that life ought to add up to something more meaningful.

A number of Yokefellow groups are conducted by clinically trained individuals, but the vast majority are led by relatively untrained personnel. A great many of them are formed by ministers since most of the groups meet in churches. However, there have been more lay persons involved as leaders than ministers since the Yokefellow material enables a qualified lay person to provide adequate leadership.

Yokefellows, Inc., of 19 Park Road, Burlingame, California, developed a tremendously effective technique years ago. Under a foundation grant the method was perfected and has been used with significant results for many years. The method consists of what are termed "spiritual growth inventories." These consist of standardized psychological tests adapted to emotional and spiritual growth. Over seventy thousand persons have participated in groups using these inventories since they were first developed. They have been utilized in churches of thirty denominations, thirty-three mental health institutions, prisons, and many universities.

The process works like this: After a group has used

a half-dozen or so Yokefellow "starting devices" over a period of six weeks, the leader sends for inventories for his group. The members take the forms home and complete them, returning them to the group leader the following week. He sends them to Yokefellows, Inc., Burlingame, California, to be processed. A series of "feedback evaluation slips" are then prepared at the center and returned to the group leader, in sealed envelopes. An evaluation slip is passed out to the members every two weeks for twenty-two weeks. The first basic inventory utilizes eleven evaluation slips. Taken every two weeks to allow for ample discussion (some groups take longer), this process lasts over five months. The cost is about a dollar a week per person. The importance and effectiveness of the slips lie in the fact that they point up, gently and nonjudgmentally, some areas of the personality in need of attention. Every person in the group is receiving similar suggestions as to where to look in their personalities for possible growth. Tension areas are pointed out. Suggestions are made as to what to read during the following week.

Also stressed is the importance of a daily quiet time, during which the suggested reading is done. The weekly evaluation slips have no doctrinal slant, but they are spiritually oriented.

God Cannot Be Limited

I refuse to believe that God works always in this way or that. Sometimes his guidance and healing seem to come directly to the individual. More often, it seems to me, the healing or blessing comes "in community," that is, as the result of relationships. In such instances it is as though God works through Fred to reach Joe, or blesses me through you, using you as a channel of love, or works through a group to bless or heal or make whole some one individual.

I am not disposed to limit God, either as to method or to the extent to which he can work. I read recently the astonishing report that teams of scientists at the

University of California at Berkeley, and in England, have made simultaneous discoveries of the evidence of "black holes in space." The black holes are believed to be invisible collapsed stars so dense that *a spoonful of material from them would weigh more than a billion tons*. Matter approaching these collapsed stars is believed to be sucked into them with great force, disappearing into infinity.

This boggles my mind, for I cannot even visualize an invisible black hole in space much less a spoonful of material that would weigh a billion tons. Yet I accept tentatively, on faith, the findings of science. And in so doing I am postulating an unbelievably powerful God. Whoever created this universe is partially unknowable, for he is infinite, and we are finite. We can never know him fully. But we can accept the statement of Jesus that "with God all things are possible" and with faith in his limitless goodness and love reach out in trust for wholeness. He wills our best. His universal cosmic laws are there to bless us, guide us, heal us, and unite us in love with our fellows. *We can trust him and his love!* Each time I have read the following, by James Dillet Freeman, I have found myself inspired to go a little farther in trusting that love:

I Sought for God

Prayer is a search for God,
I have sought for Him;
In my search, I went down many roads. I had many strange encounters. I came on many curious sights.
At last I passed through the desert of denial. In this desert I came to a place where a bush was burning.
The bush sparkled and crackled with flames but was not consumed.
While I stood gazing at this burning bush, a voice spoke out of the midst of it, "Take off your shoes, for this is holy ground."
"I must be very near to God now," I thought.
So I knelt and took off my shoes.

Barefoot I went down that road.

The way led through the plain of temptation. At first it was a land of grassy fields and crystal streams, of fruit and flowers.

But the farther I went, the barer and harder the land became, a rough country where the rocks cut and gashed my feet, so that it hurt more and more to go on. But after a while a great wind roared up the road. After the wind came an earthquake. After the earthquake came a fire. After the fire came a still small voice. The voice said, "Remove your robe, for I would see you not as you appear to be but as you are. Thus we will come to know one another."

"I must be very near to God now," I thought.

I removed my robe.

Barefoot and naked I strode through a naked land.

The road led upward through the mountains of hope—green mountains full of trees at first, but the higher I climbed the harder the way became. The rain fell cold on my nakedness.

Where the rain ceased, the snow began.

But after a while I came to the top of the mountains. On the mountaintop were three empty crosses.

Then the clouds parted and out of the clouds came a dove. The dove lit on my shoulder, and a voice said, "Leave your body, for I would make your mind one with my mind, so that there may be between you and me only a clear flow of unobstructed thinking."

"I must be very near to God now," I thought.

So on that mountaintop I left my body.

Barefoot, naked, bodiless, I sprang into the air of aspiration on unencumbered wings of thought. Like an eagle I rose up and up. A wind as from forever caught me and flung me weightless through space. The fierce fires of all the stars burned pitiless into my naked mind, stabbing it with unimagined lightnings—dreams and insights, visions and conjectures. I became bewildered and afraid. Then in this turbulence a light began to glow. In the light Something moved. This movement was as if a rainbow rippled on itself, and the waves that the rainbow formed were not only light but music, not only music but fragrance and the touch of a presence, not only a presence but clarity of thought, and the clarity of thought was perfection of mind.

Then out of that perfection of mind a voice said, "Let go of your mind, for myself and yourself must grow to be as one."

"I must be very near to God now," I thought.

So I let go of my mind.

Instantly space and time, form and formlessness, thought and non-thought vanished. Barefoot, naked, bodiless, mindless, I lay outstretched as in a vast abyss. There was no height. There was no depth. There was no beginning. There was no ending. That which I am hung in the emptiness of that which is.

Then in that absolute of silence, in that perfection empty and complete, where I was alone with the Alone, a voice said, "Give up yourself."

Then I saw that I was still alone. I had only emptiness, only silence, only seeking.

I was no nearer to God than I had been when I set out on my search.

Then I gave up myself.

Me and mine were no more. That which is more than I stood barefoot, naked, bodiless, mindless, selfless.

But where I had been, God was.

Where my self ended, love's selflessness started.

Then I saw that my bare feet are the feet of God. My naked body is the body of God.

My seeking mind is the mind of God. My lonely self is God's unselfishness seeking to give itself to me.

I saw that I was shod. I was clothed. I was in my body. I had my mind. I was myself.

I was going down the road, seeking not God, but man —not so that I might find God but so that I might lose myself in His love.[2]

NOTES

Chapter 2

1. Walter C. Langer, *The Mind of Hitler* (New York: Basic Books, 1972).
2. Sigmund Freud, *The Question of Lay Analysis* (New York: W. W. Norton, 1969).

Chapter 3

1. Desmond Morris, *The Human Zoo* (New York: McGraw Hill, Dell, 1974), p. 109.
2. Ibid., pp. 109-10.

Chapter 4

1. George Bach and Peter Wyden, *The Intimate Enemy* (New York: Avon, 1970).
2. Frederick Leboyer, *Birth Without Violence* (New York: Alfred Knopf, 1975).
3. Shana Alexander, "How to Make a Baby Smile," *Newsweek,* 31 March 1975.

Chapter 5

1. Dietrich Bonhoeffer, *The Cost of Discipleship* (New York: Macmillan, 1963), pp. 18-20. Used by permission of The SCM Press.

Chapter 6

1. Karen Horney, *Neurosis and Human Growth* (New York: W. W. Norton, 1950).
2. Emmet Fox, *Power Through Constructive Thinking* (New York. Harper and Row, 1940).

Chapter 7

1. Suzanne K. Langer, *Mind—An Essay on Human Feelings* (Baltimore, Md.: Johns Hopkins, 1972).

2. Rollo May, *Man's Search for Himself* (New York: W. W. Norton, Signet, 1967).

3. William Glasser, *Schools without Failure* (New York: Harper & Row, 1967).

4. Alvin Toffler, *Future Shock* (New York: Random House, Bantam, 1971).

5. Frederick Word Kates, *Between Dawn and Dark* (Nashville: The Upper Room, 1957).

Chapter 8

1. Toffler, *Future Shock,* p. 186.

2. Ibid., pp. 159-60.

3. Morris, *Human Zoo,* p. 191.

4. Freud, *Question of Lay Analysis* (New York: Norton Co., 1969).

5. A. Dudley Dennison, Give It to Me Straight, *Doctor* (Grand Rapids, Mich.: Zondervan, 1972).

6. Ibid.

7. Ashley Montague, *The Human Revolution* (Cleveland, Ohio: World, 1965).

8. Robert S. De Ropp, *The Master Game* (New York: Delacorte, 1968).

9. Alan Watts, *The Supreme Identity* (New York: Pantheon, 1950).

10. Ibid.

Chapter 10

1. Paul Tournier, *To Understand Each Other* (Atlanta, Ga.: John Knox Press, 1962).

Chapter 11

1. Heribert Jone, *Moral Theology* (Westminster Md.: Newman Press, 1952).

2. Augustine, *Confessions of St. Augustine* (Englewood Cliffs, N.J.: Prentice Hall, 1941).

Chapter 12

1. Karl Menninger, *The Vital Balance* (New York: Viking Press, 1967).

2. James Dillet Freeman, *Prayer, the Master Key* (New York: Doubleday, 1968), pp. 252-54.

SUGGESTED READINGS

A Scream Away from Happiness, Daniel Casriel, M.D.; Grosset and Dunlap.

The Primal Scream, Arthur Janov, Ph.D.; A Delta Book, Dell Publishing Co., Inc.

The Primal Revolution, Arthur Janov, Ph.D., A Touchstone Book; Simon and Schuster.

The Feeling Child, Arthur Janov, Ph.D., A Touchstone Book; Simon and Schuster.

Self Hypnotism, Lesle M. LeCron, Prentice-Hall, Inc.

Helping Yourself with Self Hypnotism, Frank Caprio, M.D. and Joseph R. Berger; Prentice-Hall, Inc.

The Will to Live, Arnold N. Hutschnecker, M.D., Cornerstone Library, Distributed by Simon and Schuster.

Immortality, The Scientific Evidence, Alson J. Smith, The New American Library.

The Angry Book, Theodore Rubin, M.D., Collier Books, A Division of Macmillan Publishing Co., Inc.

The Art of Understanding Yourself, Cecil G. Osborne, Zondervan Publishing House.

Low Blood Sugar, the Hidden Menace of Hypoglycemia, Clement G. Martin, M.D.; Arco Publishing Co., Inc.

Type A Behavior and Your Heart, Myer Friedman, M.D. and Ray H. Rosenman, M.D., Fawcett Publications, Inc.